HOW WILL I KNOW MY CHILDREN
WHEN I GET TO HEAVEN?

A MOTHER'S
TALES OF HOPE

GRACE VIRTUE

Aslan Publishing
2490 Black Rock Turnpike #342
Fairfield, CT 06825
www.aslanpublishing.com

The information in this publication is not designed to substitute for professional services of any kind. If any such service is required, please consult a trained professional. The Publishers and Author expressly disclaim any liability for damages resulting from inappropriate use of the information contained in this work.

Library of Congress Cataloging-in-Publication Data
Virtue, Grace.
How Will I Know My Children When I Get to Heaven? A Mother's Tales of Hope/Grace Virtue.
p. cm.

Summary: "Addresses parenting issues from the perspective of a single, immigrant mother in America. Backed by a Ph.D. in the humanities and simple, elegant writing style, the author explores topics like faith, education, body image, media usage, multiculturalism, racism, sexism, abortion, homosexuality, and other modern day challenges demonstrating the value of compassion and thoughtfulness in facing these challenges" — Provided by publisher.

ISBN 978-0-944031-19-3 (trade pbk. : alk. paper)

1. Parenting—United States.
2. Single mothers—United States. I. Title.
    HQ755.8.V563 2009
    306.874'32092–dc22
    [B]
    2009031677

Cover by thinkdesign and communications
Falls Church, Virginia
www.thinkdesign.net

Printed in the United States of America 2009

For Jihan and Jodie, and mothers and daughters everywhere.

Before you were conceived I wanted you. Before you were born I loved you. Before you were here an hour I would die for you. This is the miracle of life.

—Maureen Hawkins

Table Of Contents

Acknowledgments

Without the rich insight from my children, this book would not have been possible. I thank them earnestly for their understanding and inspiration, for their faith in me, for forgiving me even when I have been at my most uncharitable and for loving me unconditionally all the time.

I acknowledge too with tremendous gratitude the wisdom of my parents and their uncommon good sense, humility, decency and good intentions, unsurpassed and more valuable than anything material that they could ever have given me. I thank them especially for giving me a sense of family and for the values of faith, responsibility, sharing, caring and commitment that they live and effortlessly communicate to me in the process.

Thanks to my paternal grandmother for teaching me what it means to live with dignity and integrity, to my maternal grandmother who taught me to keep it real and to my siblings—Erica, Ian, Hazel, John, Lor, Dean, Neil, Sadie, Richard and Marlon, for their friendship and loyalty through the years.

Thanks to all my friends, particularly David Woods, former Associate Dean of the John H. Johnson School of Communications at Howard University, for more than a decade of warm, wonderful and caring friendship, our many conversations on the human condition and our responsibility to make it better.

Finally, thanks to mothers everywhere in the world who honor the promise implicit in their roles by unselfishly sacrificing their own needs for the welfare of their children, and thanks to the Master of the Universe, for his infinite wisdom.

Introduction

On our journeys as human beings, most of us will sometimes pause to ponder the mysteries, strangeness, complexities and unpredictability of life. For some of us, the journey is marked by pain and failures. For others, it is filled with success and good fortune beyond their wildest dreams. For nearly all of us, it is a trajectory we never quite imagined, unintended paths and lessons learned in unexpected places, taught by unsuspecting teachers.

My journey has a little of all these elements since it began over four decades ago in a remote part of the Caribbean island of Jamaica. There, the human condition could most aptly be described in degrees of deprivation and poverty: poor, poorer, poorest. My family was in the middle class: poorer. In a strange way, it was unencumbering, psychologically at least. I did not realize how poor we were until I left our small village to begin college at age 18. In the township of Mandeville, I began to meet people of different social groupings and realized that I was not supposed to be as good as many of them. Thankfully, by then my character was fully formed: I was as good as anyone else. I had a place in the world. I merely had to keep searching and working toward discovering and sustaining that place.

Among the significant stops on my journey was the idyllic campus of the University of the West Indies at Mona where I studied journalism and social science. Later, I worked in Kingston, Jamaica's capital city, and one of the world's best-equipped laboratories in the study of the human condition, good and bad. I roamed the streets in search of subjects to write about—from the vibrancy of life on North, King, Princess and Orange Streets to the dump at Riverton City; to the seat of government at Gordon House; and through the meandering curves of the countryside from Port Antonio to Savanna-La-Mar.

Among numerous interesting experiences, I was sent by my old editor, the late Carl Wint, to Madden's Funeral Home to take a look at the body of one of Jamaica's most notorious gunmen—to see if it was really him. In the few minutes that it took me to get there, permission was abruptly rescinded by the funeral home, ostensibly under orders from the Ministry of National Security. Still, I remember the piercing stares of the onlookers as I arrived at the building in the company-owned car and the involuntary shiver up my spine as I attempted to navigate one of the strangest, most macabre experiences of my life. On more pleasant occasions, I was presented to Queen Elizabeth II and I had the privilege of being in the same room with Winnie and Nelson Mandela.

From Kingston, it was on to Howard University, Washington D.C., where I earned two graduate degrees on scholarships while raising my two daughters whom, for the purpose of this book, I have re-named Alya and Ilsa. Alya, the older, was born in January, 1991 and Ilsa, November, 1992. They came to the United States in 1997, at ages six and four, a year after I started my studies in 1996. As it was in Jamaica, I would find myself wandering the corridors of power in the United States, even sitting in President Bill Clinton's chair in the Cabinet Room at the White House.

I have shaken a few hands and avoided others. I have laughed much at some of life's absurdities and I have cried at others. I have sometimes worked hard; I have slacked off at others. I have been overwhelmed at times and infinitely underwhelmed at others. I have been blissfully fulfilled at times. At other times, the emptiness seemed like a black hole with neither end nor beginning.

Ultimately, none of my life's experiences have been as precious, as rich, as deep or as meaningful as those I have shared with my daughters, both of whom have proven more adept at getting to the heart of a matter than any teacher I have ever had. Always, they are perceptive, precise, blissfully undiplomatic and completely without rancor. They have kept me focused whenever I seemed in danger of losing sight of my goals. They have picked me up from the depths of unbelief and unworthiness; they have yanked me back from the precipice of arrogance and anger, forcing me always to choose my better self.

The lessons from our lives, recounted in this book, cover some of our experiences roughly over the course of 11 years. With the exception of Chapter 21, "Of Perfect Love," prompted in part by a question Alya asked at age five, the passages are prompted by incidents in the United States. Overall, the passages focus more on themes rather than chronology, which means that the children may be older in earlier passages and younger in later ones. Further, they are descriptive, rather than prescriptive, intending more to compare notes with the millions of women with whom I share the sacred bond of motherhood. They are especially relevant to those of us who are torn between our professional ambitions and our desire to be good mothers, to those who have the courage and the wherewithal to chuck the career and just be "Mommy," and to those who must battle poverty, marginalization and prejudices in the quest to raise their children alone. Mostly, these lessons are designed to provide a moment of pause on the insight of the poet, Khalil Gibran:

Your children are not your children
They are the sons and daughters of Life's longing for itself.
They come through you but not from you, and
Though they are with you yet they belong not to you.
You may give them your love but not your thoughts,
For they have their own thoughts.
You may house their bodies but not their souls
For their souls dwell in the house of tomorrow
Which you cannot visit, not even in your dreams.
You may strive to be like them, but seek not to make them like you.
For life goes not backward nor tarries with yesterday.

ONE

Peace, Be Still

Compassion is the keen awareness of the interdependence of all things.

—Thomas Merton

I figure I could program the DVD or the VCR if I read the manual slowly and carefully.

My daughters, Alya and Ilsa, do it without reading the manual.

I have never put on Rollerblades, or is it roller skates?

Whatever it is, my daughters walk around in them or on them almost like they were no different from their sneakers.

I am morbidly afraid of lizards and most crawling things.

To my daughters, they are God's creatures—part of the ecosystem that is integral to the survival of all life on the planet.

I would probably die if I ever held a caterpillar in my hand.

My girls bring them in the house, in their hands, just to see how scared I really am.

I don't know how to swim.

For them, summer is not summer without a pool nearby. Swim, float, whatever. They must be in the pool. I watch from the side with a book.

I still do not know how to ride a bike.

Well, my daughters just find that funny. They have offered to teach me as soon as I am ready.

I was twenty-one years old before I ever went on an airplane.

At the security checkpoints, they heartlessly ignore me and, with a hundred eye rolls, entreat me to go home now; they will find their way to the concourse. After all, haven't they been doing this since the first or second grade?

My daughters had as much to teach me as I had to teach them, came the belated realization. It was not quite how I had envisaged it when I first became a mother. Then, I thought I would be the master teacher, teaching them everything: how to read, how to count, how to cross the street, how to navigate the challenges of being girls, women and eventually mothers, and most importantly how to be decent human beings.

I soon caught on to a new dynamic and let myself go, let myself learn the lessons that my children had to teach me about the world, about life, about how to be a decent human being. After all, they are growing into a world that I am growing out of; there will be much that they will embrace that I will not even understand. We do not grow parallel to our children. We decline as they ascend. This is the nature of human existence—the circle of life. It would serve me well, I soon realized, to open my heart and my mind to the recognition that they too are my life's teachers and the lessons they had to teach were as deep as they were eternal; that implicit in their youth was a new knowledge and a unique brand of wisdom that I would need to guide me along the way.

A great big lesson in patience and compassion came one day when I had been at my worst, physically, emotionally and spiritually. From out of nowhere, a late spring storm blew into our neighborhood in Glenmont, Maryland. Big and ugly, it charged in just around the time the children were getting out of Glenallan Elementary School, about three-quarters of a mile away from our apartment. All around, the trees were bending, twisting and shimmying in a fast, frenzied dance. Thunder pounded through the heavens and streaks of lightning made frighteningly beautiful golden patterns against the black clouds.

The girls had not made it home. They were somewhere out in the storm.

On a good day, the walk home from school was a pleasant fifteen minutes if they did not dawdle, and they rarely did. Emerging from the school premises, they simply had to cross the street where busy Randolph Road meets Glenallan Avenue. This they did under the watchful eyes of two crossing guards. After that, it was just a matter of skipping between the red brick buildings interspersed with groves of stately Sycamores until they reached our building on Glenmont Circle.

In the springtime, the woods are incandescently lovely. Sunlight filters through the leaves, creating mythical patterns on the grass and forest beds below, reminding me of paradise and of every pretty song I know. Come fall each year, and I am awed all over again at the transformation of the leaves from shimmering greens to countless shades of warm mustards, browns and golds. Even the bare craggy branches in winter had its own special appeal that over time, this child of the sun had grown to love.

Big, stately old trees have their disadvantage, however. The wild rhapsody triggered by the wind and rain could easily bring some of them down, to the detriment of power lines and errant humans below. Plus, there was the lightning, coldly lovely and deadly, zigzagging against huge puffs of angry clouds. It did not matter that lightning strikes were few and far between, on this day, I was afraid anyway. I grabbed my coat and hurried toward the door.

In my mind, I saw my mother as clear as if it were yesterday, making a similar run in the woods above our house in rural Jamaica. We were at home, one Saturday afternoon, when the sun disappeared beneath suddenly thick, dark clouds, an ominous warning that a thunderstorm was near. Ten of her eleven children were playing in the front yard or just lazing on the verandah; one, my younger brother, John, was missing.

—w—

John is child number five and my mother's second son. I still remember him as a dear dimpled little boy with soft dusky skin, the color of the sand at Alligator Pond Bay. His hair was straight and shiny, a genetic throwback to some East Indian ancestry on my father's side. With a ready wit and quick smile and a near photographic memory, he was a clear favorite at home and among the extended family of cousins, aunts and uncles and grandparents.

Of course, no one could forget that it was upon John's birth that my mother became gravely ill and was hospitalized. I was around four at the time and it seemed to me that my mother was in the hospital forever and for an equally long time that my father awkwardly played the roles my mother would normally—cooking, washing, making sure we bathed before going to bed at night. It must have seemed that way to my mother too because, at some point, she checked herself out of the hospital and came home to her children, including the baby whom everyone called John-John.

My mother soon became ill again. The doctor put her back in the hospital and told her she would die if she left again before she was properly discharged and if she had any more children. She listened to the doctor on one count only; she stayed until he told her she was properly healed. In the ensuing years, she had six more children.

Thus, John-John in his earliest years was raised for a while by his father and four siblings, ranging in age from four to nine. He still missed his mother. He clung to his pet, a black-and-white dog named Tiger, and to his favorite item of clothing, a little brown nylon baseball cap with a teddy bear at the front.

Years later, on a late August day, John, then a strapping teenager, had gone deep into the woods to tend our tiny herd of goats and perhaps shoot a few birds with his slingshot. As the lightning crisscrossed the sky, my mother kept her eyes toward the heavens as if trying to gauge its mood—trying to decide how to respond to the magnificence of its growing anger. She looked and looked. Then, without a word, she took off running away from the safety of the house. I watched her run uphill as fast as she could until she turned off the road and her brightly colored dress disappeared into the woods along the path my brother had taken.

She emerged later, her son towering over her five-foot frame. Water dripped from their clothes and faces but the smile on my mother's face was one of deep satisfaction. Her son was safely back home.

—m—

What man of you having an hundred sheep, if he lose one of them, doth not leave the ninety and nine in the wilderness, and go after that which is lost, until he find it?[1]

I did not have ninety-nine more, nor ten more, or even one more. Two was the sum total of my flock and it was out there in the storm.

My left leg hurt badly. The pain, of uncertain origin, was years old, present and searing. I half limped, half ran as fast as I could along the route the children would normally take, expecting to meet them around every next bend.

The school custodians, dressed in their bright orange ponchos, were still in the crosswalk when I reached the intersection of Randolph Road and Glenallan Avenue.

"Have you seen my girls?" I asked May Ling, the friendly Korean woman who had been the guard for all four years since the girls had started Glenallan. I routinely stopped to talk to her and as if sensing my struggles, she watched out for the girls for me, even bringing a bag with clothes and shoes she thought we could use one day. We didn't quite need it, but I was grateful anyway.

That evening, she too was perplexed as to why she had not seen them. Her perplexity fueled my anxiety, and I began a painful run down the narrow asphalt walkway toward the school. And, there they were, beside a tiny canal, two little figures crouching close to the ground in the pouring rain.

"What are you doing?" I yelled.

Two pairs of dark eyes looked innocently back at me from beneath red and blue hoods as water dripped down their faces.

"What are you doing?" I yelled again, this time stomping my right foot for good measure. "How often do I tell you that you must hurry home in time to catch the guards in the crosswalk? How often do I tell you to hurry home out of the storms?"

I was loud.

I was angry.

I was at my ranting best.

No answer.

I went quiet even as the rage roared inside my head louder than the howling wind. I had every reason to be angry, I told myself. First, their disobedience; second, their foolhardiness; and third, their refusal to even grant me the courtesy of a response.

The pain in my foot blazed as hot as the build-up of anger, hurt, disappointment and self-pity sitting on my chest and threatening to overcome me. It was compounded by the run in the wind and rain to find the girls, but they were not the source of it. I knew that, and I struggled to control my anger.

It was all about how much I had given up in my pursuit of more—my career back home; proximity to friends and family; Cheryl, my helper-friend, who washed, ironed and cleaned my house in the daytime, bathed and fed my daughters after school and stayed with them until I got home in the evenings.

It was about the security of citizenship and nationhood that become so much more important when the rules, norms and laws of your new land tell you so clearly that you do not belong.

It was about the unexpected, unintended path of single parenthood and the knowledge that the children's safety and well-being was mostly all on me—the knowledge that I was their primary anchor against the storms of life and, in many cases, their only anchor.

It was about what I could possibly have done and how much farther I could or could not have gone, if I had not found them bending down there on the narrow path near the wetland, a tiny area of trees and shrubs created by Alya's fourth-grade class.

It was about the magnitude of my relief at finding them and how much I wanted to cry, scream my relief.

It was about an overwhelming need to cry for mothers everywhere who must bear the brunt of child bearing and then child rearing, alone.

And, it was about a sudden fury at aloneness, ambition, broken dreams and those that I still clung to—those that were keeping me here in the United States, far away from home.

The storm raging around me could barely match the one inside my head. I felt my body go limp and I knew I was seconds away from a complete meltdown.

Suddenly, Ilsa spoke up. "Well," she began in that way too grown-up tone of voice she had. "We were helping the earthworms to get across the puddle. It was pretty clear that they were going to drown, so we decided to help them."

I looked down and, sure enough, there were a number of earthworms, all heading in the same direction, away from the wetland and toward the opening of the narrow canal on the other side of the path.

—〰—

E arthworms are not the most attractive creatures. As a child, I had often wondered what the purpose of some creatures was. Earthworms fell squarely in that category. I found it especially nauseating that their bodies could break in halves and continue on as two worms instead of a dead one.

As an adult, I grew to learn that they are invaluable to the ecosystem. By consuming dead leaves, they break down old vegetation into smaller, simpler parts that can be reused by other organisms. So, they are ugly, but they have a vital part to play in maintaining the earth's natural balance. More and more, I had grown to appreciate just how important that was.

While I have always loved the birds, the ocean, the trees and flowers, my intellectual appreciation of the environment and the dynamism of its many components deepened considerably in my undergraduate years, influenced by one of my professors, Aggrey Brown.

It was he who introduced me to Chief Seattle's timeless and profoundly moving statement on the environment in response to the U.S. government's demand that he sell lands belonging to his Indian tribe:

Every part of this earth is sacred to my people; every shining pine needle, every sandy shore. Every mist in the dark wood, every clearing and every insect is holy in the memory of my people. The sap, which courses through the trees, carries the memories of my people. The perfumed flowers are our sisters. We are part of the earth, and the earth is part of us. The deer, the horse, the great eagles are our brothers... All things are connected.[2]

My New Age children, far more in tune with the environment than I had been when I was their age, had already embraced the principle of "all things are connected" even if they were yet to hear of Chief Seattle.

I looked at the worms again and back at them. I saw the questions in Alya's lovely brown eyes and recalled the times in the past when I had tried to kill some wayward insect with household spray, only to hear her pleading gently: "Please don't kill it, Mommy; just put it outside."

I took a long deep breath, drew both of them into my arms and tried to explain how even compassion and love needed to be tempered with wisdom and common sense.

"You know, it would be okay if Planet Earth lost a few earthworms, but it would not be okay if this tree toppled over on you guys. It would not be okay to lose either of you. Your lives are infinitely more valuable than that of five or six earthworms."

They nodded in agreement and I hailed their innate goodness. My children were good people. They were sweet and warm and kind and compassionate, qualities to be valued regardless of how hard the storms raged.

The rain and the wind receded and a silver lining was emerging on the fringe of that great mass of black clouds just over our shoulders. The chatter inside my head was subsiding too, and in my heart a growing peace.

TWO

The End of the Road

We are not human beings on a spiritual journey.
We are spiritual beings on a human journey.

—Stephen Covey

I am old, jaded even, compared to an eight-year-old girl. This was partly why I did not give a second thought to the old man sitting on the grass on the street corner; the one who caught Ilsa's attention and triggered questions in her head to which she demanded answers—from me.

We were walking through the Glenmont Shopping Center in Maryland where we lived, her hand safely tucked in mine. She was eight going on nine and suddenly tall and lovely. Holding her hand now was a friendship thing—a far cry from the early days when it was a well-needed measure of restraint.

She prattled away happily. I listened absently, responding with an effortless "uh-huh" or "uh-uh" and she seemed content with the knowledge that I was *hearing* her, at least. Soon, we stopped at the intersection, the inevitable fork in the road, and waited for the light to signal that it was safe to continue straight across.

Suddenly, she tugged at my hand, demanding my full attention. I followed her perplexed eyes across the street to where an old man sat on the grass, a small miscellany of clothes, plastic, paper and cans scattered around him. He had the dirty, unkempt and haphazardly put together look of the chronically homeless.

It was not a common sight in our pleasant suburban neighborhood. Nonetheless, on my own, I would have passed the old man with no more than a cursory glance. After all, I was used to homelessness, first in Kingston where I had lived, and next in the District of Columbia, particularly in the Shaw neighborhood near Howard University. It did not shock me anymore, and to the extent that I did not see myself as able to do anything about it, I passed the homeless by. On that day though, my daughter forced me not just to look but to think about it for a little while.

"What happened to him?" she asked.

My brain was slow to respond. I had been deep in thoughts, contemplating the challenges in my life and the numerous obstacles to surmount—such as how I was going to come up with next month's rent; how I was going to keep a roof over our heads and four walls around us; how I was going to continue to hold unto that tiny capsule within which contained our worldly goods, and in many ways, our hopes and dreams. Our tiny apartment was home, but only as long as I could pay the rent.

—⟋⟍—

Four years before, in the fall of 1996, I took leave of my journalism job in Jamaica to pursue a master's degree in mass communication at Howard University. I left my children Alya, then five and Ilsa, three, at home with their father, my sister and my helper-friend while I pursued the two-semester program. I needed to do it, I believed, to make myself more competitive—to get ahead; to free myself from the cycle of paycheck to paycheck and ultimately to give my children a better life. I finished in the spring of 1997. The children took their first trip to the United States to attend my graduation. A few days later, I returned with them to the sultry heat of Kingston.

By the fall of that same year, I decided to return to pursue a doctorate, this time with the children, and their father. A year later, the family unit would be fractured. Their father and I separated and I was on my own with the children. I determined to stay, complete my program and return home, the mantra of many immigrants to the United States.

It doesn't matter whether home is Mexico, El Salvador, Jamaica, Ghana or some war-torn places of the world. Many of us arrive in America intending to go back one day. Moreover, upon arrival, we find that the connection to the homeland is even stronger than we thought. We miss our extended families, the native food and traditions and the often simpler lives in the folk societies from which we come. For those of us from the Caribbean, the craving for a glimpse of the sea, the mountains and the vibrancy of island culture often morph into a deep pain—a constant longing to go back, which for one reason or another can become an impossibility.

Most importantly, we arrive in America to discover that life is hard, much harder than we ever imagined. The fear of not having enough to pay the bills which arrive with remarkable precision every month, is a constant. It was especially so for a single mother of two dear little girls whom I believed deserved only the best. But here I was not even allowed the luxury of working two or three jobs to earn some extra income. My status as an international student made me ineligible to work even at McDonald's, regardless of how long I lived in the country. It was a shock.

—w—

Before her insistent tug on my arm, I treated Ilsa's chatter as pleasing background sound. It gave me pleasure, but it was nothing I needed to pay attention to. Now she was giving me something to think about, demanding answers about a life of which I knew nothing.

I struggled to give her something not merely to shut her up, but to do justice to the fragility and complexity of the human condition as she was witnessing it on that glorious spring day. She was talking again, long before I could frame a coherent answer.

"Eh, Mommy? Eh Mommy? How does someone end up homeless and lonely like that?"

My heart smiled, fleetingly, ironically. For, right then, I could have told her that I was one tiny little paycheck away from homelessness myself. That I lived on the edge of a deep, dark fear that one slight, unexpected twist of fate and I could be right there—on a busy street corner, my children and my worldly goods at my feet, unnoticed by old, jaded passersby. Instead, I paused and searched deeper for answers to questions that were about more than a single old man on the grassy edge of a busy suburban street.

"Eh Mommy? Eh, Mommy? How is it possible for a life to go so terribly wrong?"

The questions were filled with urgency and a stirring poignancy for a mother who had seen, felt sadness and heartbreak—a mother keenly aware of how easy it was for dreams to go awry, and life to go terribly wrong.

Across America, the National Alliance to End Homelessness says three-and-a half million people experience homelessness every year, many of them in the District of Columbia, the nation's capital. I thought about some of those I had seen on the Avenue of the Disconsolate— the strip between Florida Avenue and the Shaw Metro Station near Howard University.

They were everywhere, clothed in varying expressions of bewilderment and defeat. I closed my eyes and conjured up images of one of its more permanent residents, a woman with dull, lifeless eyes, dressed all the time in the same pale green sweat pants, her braids hanging down her face beneath a white ski cap with a double-roll at her hairline.

"Ma'am, a quarter please?" she begged all the time. The look in her eyes said her tenuous existence hung together by an uncertain string of quarters—that the people hustling by represented nothing more to her.

What was the story of her life? What quirky twist of fate had left her begging on a filthy city street? There had to be a story, just as there was one behind my ill-fitting blue jeans, ubiquitous pony tail, black leather bag crammed with books, weighing down my shoulder, far away from home, always hurrying. Always hurrying.

Then there was the woman I met in Silver Spring. I saw her first near the intersection of East West Highway and Colesville Road and another time near Spring Street and Georgia Avenue, meandering in and out of the traffic at the stoplight.

She was a mixed race woman—Asian and black—in her late thirties or early forties. Her skin was an unhealthy pale yellow, and she had long, loose black hair with still a hint of shine. She wore lemon yellow pants and a black cardigan. I had never seen a homeless person who looked like her in Jamaica nor in the District of Columbia where the homeless were nearly always black. The do-gooder in me wanted to give her a dollar; the journalist wanted to hear her story. I crossed Spring Street and called out to her.

"Hey," I said leaning against the wall near the bus stop.

"Hi," she answered.

"How are you?" I asked cautiously. She responded with a half-smile and a shrug.

I tried again.

"It's kind of busy here. Aren't you afraid you might get hit?"

As if to validate the question the southbound Y-8 bus swooshed by, enveloping us in a fast-moving gust of warm air. I shrank back against the wall.

"I'll be fine," she said dismissively.

I resorted to the oldest trick in the book.

"You are so beautiful," I said. "Why are you on the street begging?"

She leaned against the wall next to me and began to talk.

Not long before, she used to get dressed in nice clothes in the mornings and go to her job. She had an average life like any number of people in the United States. Then, the unexpected happened. She was diagnosed with kidney disease and needed dialysis almost immediately. The treatment took her away from her job for long hours and soon she lost her job. With the job went her health insurance. Without insurance, her treatment became less certain and her illness worsened. No one would hire her in that condition. She lost her home and her average life.

I gave her all the money I had—a one dollar bill and sixty-five cents. I had a transfer to get home, enough food in the cupboard and my credit card to see me through until the next day when I would collect my three hundred and sixty-five dollar graduate assistant stipend.

I saw her a few more times from the windows of the metro buses I rode. She seemed to be losing weight everywhere but from her stomach; her eyes retreated farther and farther back inside her head, and then, I did not see her anymore.

—⚉—

I saw homeless people often in Jamaica, numerous broken lives, scattered across urban centers from Negril to Morant Point. They were often abused, set upon. They ate at the whim of strangers. They lived at the mercy of the wind, rain and heat.

Then, there were the men at Curphey Home, a place for veterans of World Wars I and II, located not far from where I grew up in the cool hills of South Manchester. The men had fought as British Citizens in the wars and were being taken care of by the Jamaica Legion, an affiliate of the British Commonwealth Ex-Services League. I remember one "old soldier" especially. I often saw him on my way to and from school, staggering back in the direction of the home on his way from the village bar. White-haired and ruddy-cheeked, he was always drunk and always crying, a river of tears that went on and on.

Technically, the men were not homeless, just too traumatized and broken by war to put the pieces of their lives back together again. It was the same with many of America's homeless veterans of the Vietnam War and now the Iraq War.

Slowly, I began to explain to my daughter how easy it is for lives to go horribly wrong.

"Some people end up lonely and homeless because they make bad choices. They gamble, use drugs, drop out of school. They break the law and end up in jail. It is hard to get back on your feet after that. But this is not true for most people. Some people get sick and lose their jobs, or others just have bad experiences that they just can't get over."

She was looking at me, her eyes wide and serious. I continued talking.

"It's easy to think that people end up lonely and homeless because they are lazy but most of the time, this is not true. It is just easier for us to believe this because that way, we do not have to feel responsible for helping them. So, many of them end up like that at the side of the road."

I did not know the old man and I had no idea why he was there, but I did know that, once upon a time, he was a baby. He likely had a mother who sang to him and rocked him on her breast. He might have been, and may still be a husband, a father, a brother or an uncle. His story, like that of the majority of homeless people, was not necessarily one of failure or sloth, but it was certainly one of deep, human suffering.

"What can I do to make sure that I do not end up that way?"

The question resounded in my ears and everywhere in the urgency in her voice. Already, she was smart, hard-working, well-grounded and doing everything right. When her story is written in the book of life, it should rightfully be one of great success and stirring inspiration. Yet, I know that there are no guarantees in life, especially when "success" itself so often leads to disaster and heartbreak. Then, there are those of us who, battered by life's vagaries, may never literally end up on the side of the road, but in spite of our best efforts will find ourselves at the end of life's road with all of our lovely dreams broken and scattered at our feet. As someone living far away from home, without even the right to belong, I was all too keenly aware of how easily that could happen.

I hugged her tightly.

"Keep on doing what you are doing now. Work hard in school, and like my mama used to say, stay on the straight and narrow. Avoid bad company, avoid drugs of all kinds, and always think carefully about whatever you do. Sometimes, all it takes is one bad decision to throw us off track completely."

She nodded and I sent up a silent prayer, because I knew that only so much of it is up to us—that there, goes any of us, but for the grace of God.

THREE

Stranger Danger

If you want your children to turn out well, spend twice as much time with them, and half as much money.

—Abigail Van Buren (Dear Abby)

Don't talk to strangers.
Never open the door to strangers, especially if you are alone at home.
Never get in a car with anyone you don't know.
If you find yourself in a situation that makes you uncomfortable,
run away if you can; it is better to feel silly later than to be sorry.

Like most mothers, I admonished my daughters every day. After a while, I thought they understood, and I assumed they agreed. Soon enough, I would realize that I thought so only because I failed to fully appreciate that they were not miniature versions of me, but young children who look at life through their own lenses, minus the experiences and judgment that come only with adulthood.

Half seriously, half mockingly, they took to finishing my sentences every time I began to go over the rules. Their attitude said they thought I was paranoid but they would humor me anyway. I agreed that I was paranoid, just a little, but it was healthy since it helped to keep everyone safe.

Moreover, my paranoia was well founded. The number of itinerant laborers moving into our apartment complex seemed to be exploding by the day. The signs were everywhere in the empty beer bottles and fast-food packaging left on the staircase overnight. More and more, I seemed to be stepping over folks resting on the stairs, on my way to my unit. It terrified me that in my absence, the girls had to be stepping over people to get inside our apartment, or that someone was watching them take their keys out of their backpacks to let themselves in.

Then, there is the big picture beyond where I lived—the photographs of missing children on the little flyers that I get with the mail mostly every day followed by a computerized age progression image underneath the words: "Have you seen me?"

In the United States and all over the world, children go missing daily—sometimes inexplicably so. This phenomenon speaks as much to their special vulnerability as it does to a complex problem to which there are seemingly no real solutions. Children are taken from their homes or snatched off the streets or playgrounds, often by relatives and many times by strangers. Snatching by strangers are referred to as stereotypical kidnappings and are usually worst-case scenarios. Children are typically taken more than fifty miles from home, are missing for more than twenty-four hours, are taken with the intention of being sexually abused, held permanently or killed, or a ransom is demanded for their safe return.[3]

In my former life as a journalist in Jamaica, cases of missing people—children in particular, were among the issues that haunted me most. Coupled with the shock of having "it" happen to them, was the frustration of family members coping with presumed tragedy, their inability to do much about it, and the ineptitude and even callousness of the police sometimes.

In some cases, missing persons return home alive. Often there are situations where people opt to leave home without telling anyone of their whereabouts or where their children are taken by relatives without the knowledge of their custodial parent or guardian. The remains of too many are discovered in the inevitable "shallow grave," or families, forced by the passage of years, concede that their loved one is gone forever, vanished into some great unyielding unknown. In many instances, those who went missing, stayed missing.

One thing was certain: In Jamaica, there would be no army of police or volunteers searching the mountains and valleys as often happens in missing persons cases in the United States. The unavailability of resources and the fact that the police do not take reports of missing people seriously enough, preclude such responses.

Even though more than a decade has passed, I still find myself mulling the outcome of missing cases I had worked. For example, five-year-old Krysta Gayle from St. Thomas, Jamaica, disappeared from a path by the side of her house while her mother sat a few yards away. Family members say one minute the little girl was walking toward them on the track, the next she had vanished.

By the time I reached St. Thomas, pen and notebook in hand, Krysta's mother had been hospitalized, suffering from an emotional breakdown. Then a young mother myself, I became obsessed with protecting my daughters from any such fate. It was even more so when I left Jamaica to attend school and became deeply aware that here, on the vast continental USA, with all its resources, searching for two missing black children could so easily become the proverbial needle in a haystack.

The size of America frightened me in many ways. It was unlike my island culture where I could walk the streets, go in and out of little shops, flag down passing cars and inquire of anyone and everyone if they had seen anything and if so where and when. Jamaica has few resources and the police often do not always care but in America, it is quite easy to get from Maryland to Texas or California. How far could I possible go in search of Ilsa and Alya if they turned up missing?

—〰—

My daughters were latchkey kids, to my dismay, letting themselves into the empty apartment until I came home from work or school. At no point in my life did I imagine raising them alone, far away from friends and family, nor had I envisaged a protracted period of my life where I was under-employed and therefore without the resources to provide adequate care for them.

As a graduate student, I earned between seven and eight thousand dollars a year in stipend in exchange for teaching two freshman classes. As the only form of employment allowed on my student visa, the money was my one reliable source of income from which my household bills had to be paid. There was absolutely no wriggle room as far as fulfilling my obligations to the program were concerned. I had to fulfill my duties in order to get the stipend and I had to attend my classes toward the completion of my program.

What would be the point of graduate school if I lost my children along the way? Lost them to the streets? To the big old world with sundry gaping holes? To some creepy stranger who watched them enough to know when they were home alone? To someone who saw them trying to let themselves in and followed them inside?

I raced home as quickly as I could every day but Ilsa, still in elementary school, would still make it home ten or fifteen minutes before I did most days. Young as my daughters were, I had to rely on their understanding and obedience to help me keep them safe.

Things had been going fine, I thought, until my sense of security in our arrangements was unexpectedly shattered one day by Ilsa, then eight years old.

I reached home one evening, turned the key in the lock and entered the apartment as usual. I could tell Ilsa was already home, judging from the little mound of books and bags on the living room floor. It was not time yet time for Alya, then in the sixth grade, to get home. At least, I could open the door for her.

I breathed a sigh of relief. One more day safely negotiated so far.

On cue, Ilsa came charging out of her room, excitedly waving a package.

"I signed for you," she said proudly, holding up a brown UPS envelope.

I stopped where I was, closed my eyes and breathed deeply. Rule number one—never open the door to a stranger—had been breached, evidenced by her own declaration and the envelope she was waving so proudly.

"I thought the rule was that you don't open the door to strangers especially when you are alone. Isn't that what we agreed on?"

She looked at me, crestfallen. After all, she had done a most responsible thing. She had opened the door, signed for my package and put it away safely until I got home.

"But Mommy, I knew who it was," she countered earnestly. "It was the UPS guy. The UPS guy is not a stranger!"

My heart sank further. All along, I thought they understood. Now, it was clear to me that she did not quite get it. Or, she thought she was grown enough to make a judgment as to who was or was not a stranger. She was wrong. Was there a way to convince her of that?

The thoughts churned in my head. It was not hard to see her logic. After all, the "UPS guy" was a familiar sight. She would have seen the same brown uniformed person beside the same brown truck around the neighborhood before, and she would have seen someone who look like him in countless television commercials. Perhaps too, the same brown-uniformed guy had delivered a package to our apartment before. He was always pleasant and polite—a hard-working man doing a legitimate and very important job. He was not a scary stranger who would do anyone harm. In the construct of a child, this generic "UPS guy" was not a stranger at all.

But to a mother whose emotions were always at the intersection of the purest love for her children, bright dreams for their future and guilt and anxiety about them being on their own—if even for a few minutes—the little girl, still holding the envelope, had just told whoever the stranger in the uniform was, that she was home alone. What if he had been a pervert or worse?

I sat on the sofa, pulled her down on my leg and explained why the UPS guy was a stranger and why it would have been okay if he had taken the package back and returned another day.

"There is absolutely nothing in that package that is more important than your safety," I told her. "He could easily have come back tomorrow or another day, or I could have picked it up from their office downtown. Do you understand?"

She nodded and I reminded myself that she was not being disobedient; she was just a little girl looking at the world through the lens of her limited experience. In the meantime, I had no right to ask anything more of her regardless of my circumstances.

As she wandered back to her room, her ego still a little bruised, I reflected on what brought me to this place and just how my own thinking had evolved—how I had reconfigured my dreams at a point in my life when I did not have a chance in hell of living them.

Early on, much of my ambitions had been about chasing an education and a career that I thought would give my children a shot at a better life, with all the things I never had and the ascendant status that, ostensibly, comes with material arrival. I hoped too, that climbing that mountain and fulfilling a dream that had seemed unattainable, would bring me some level of fulfillment and inspire the girls to fight to fulfill their own aspirations. Every difficult decision I made had been influenced by the drive to ensure that they would have so much more than I had, including the freedom to live their lives the way they wanted.

But after an investment of four-and-a-half years in graduate school and finding gainful employment, I found myself wishing more and more that in their earlier years at least, I could have been there to take them to the park more often—to watch them slide through the tunnels on the playground, to ride with them on the beautiful old carousel in Wheaton Regional Park, to chase them as they chased the geese and ducks, to stop with them and smell the roses much more often than I did.

As they grew older, I wanted to be the quintessential soccer mom, contentedly driving a minivan with dirty tennis shoes on the back seats; driving them myself to basketball, music lessons or dance, instead of putting them in the back of a cab with a stranger or making the difficult decision not to send them at all. Most importantly, I wished I could have been home to greet them when they got home from school, just as my mother did for me for more than twelve years. In the grand scheme of things, it was a simple dream, but as it turned out, the most unattainable of all. Not much would change anytime soon so we simply had to settle for the equilibrium rather than the dream.

The desire to be there for them, physically and emotionally, was multiplied a million times, every time I heard media stories of children attacked in their own homes by predators who studied their routines and laid in wait for them. A few such cases in our Silver Spring neighborhood in 2004 triggered a new round of introspection and anxiety, as did the case of a young Florida girl, eleven-year-old Carly Brucia, abducted on camera as she took a shortcut home from a friend's house. I shed many silent tears for her and for my own girls, both of them then very near her age.

Now, I know that I will never earn enough money or acquire enough material things to compensate for lost time with my children. It was a sad realization for me, but what's done is already done. However, it is a liberating feeling as well for a mother, or an individual, to recognize, however belatedly, the things that truly matter in life, and those that do—only just a little.

FOUR

This Is My Body

I promise you caring, the love of your family
I promise you all I can give
To help you become the best person you can
And to live the best life you can
I'll let you know my thoughts, as you form your own
I'll help you know the world too,
And when the day comes, that you stand on your own
I'll love and accept you as you

—Author Unknown

It was hard to find privacy in the small two-bedroom, one-bathroom apartment where we lived but I was never overly concerned. I shared my life with two young girls who would one day become women and there was not much that I wanted to hide from them—not even my body with its residual evidence of painful pregnancies and childbirth.

I stepped out of the shower one day just as Ilsa poked her head around the bathroom door. Silently, she stared for a moment as if something about my body had caught her attention for the first time. I looked back inquiringly. After all, she had seen me naked before.

"Why are your breasts so flat?" she asked finally, an incredulous note to her voice as though she was noticing for the first time that they were different from what she thought they were supposed to be.

They had never bothered me before, but the critical note in her voice was intimidating enough for me to try and rationalize it.

"Well, you know, I have you and Alya. I breastfed both of you for as long as I could. It changed my body …"

She would have none of it. "You could have stopped breastfeeding me earlier you know," she said, the same incredulous note to her voice. "Seriously, I would not have minded!"

Laughter bubbled up inside my body and spilled out like sprays from a waterfall. I did not laugh often enough and here was a heaven-sent opportunity for some of life's best medicine. Of course, it was not funny that my body was somewhat misshapen compared to the nubile condition of a young maiden like her. What was funny was that this same little girl was a partial beneficiary of my undoing. She was conceived inside my body. My stomach stretched and stretched to accommodate her growing form for nine months and upon her birth, I decided to breastfeed—to give her the very best start in life. Now, here she was rejecting the noble choice I thought I had made and finding me wanting too.

She was not done. In fact, what she saw as my nonchalance only annoyed her more.

"At least you would have still had some use for them,' she declared angrily. "Look at them! They are just like two flat tires!"

I laughed harder.

I had long accepted that, upon childbirth, my body had changed for the worse; that the long, lean form of my teen years and early twenties had gone for good; that my breasts drooped, that I had too much fat on my stomach and stretch marks where lovely smooth cinnamon skin used to be.

Fortunately, or unfortunately, I am not a Hollywood star nor am I among the wealthy of any category. If I were, perhaps I would consider more cosmetic surgery—an abdominoplasty, for example, to remove excess fat and skin, and tighten the muscles of the abdominal wall some

more. I had already had one surgery, which I thought was absolutely
necessary. The results were not great. I would need much more work for
my stomach to even come close to my pre-motherhood days.

Maybe I would even entertain the idea of a procedure to raise
and reshape my breasts—a breast lift or mastopexy. I probably wouldn't
do it though, because of possible side effects which may include scarring,
infection, inaccurate repositioning of the nipples, and permanent loss
of feeling in the nipples and breast. Still, it is among the most popular
surgeries in America's multi-billion-dollar cosmetic industry.

Since I could barely afford daycare, I figured my body would
remain just the way it was and I would have to grow old "gracefully"—
whether I wanted to or not. The acuity of the Serenity Prayer was
my comfort:

> *God, grant me the serenity to accept*
> *the things I cannot change*
> *The courage to change those I can*
> *And the wisdom to know the difference.*

Moreover, generations of women before me, including my
mother, grandmothers and great-grandmothers, lived long and happy
lives with their bloated tummies and sagging breasts after giving birth
to numerous children. They knew nothing of Hollywood nor would they
have been privy to its make-believe notions of beauty or felt any pressure
to even attempt to attain its fantastic standards. Their husbands mostly
stayed with them, loved them anyway and continued to have healthy sex
lives—if the number of children were anything to go by.

I figured that my life, as far as my body was concerned, would
be mostly the same, except for what I could change through diet and
exercise. I never dreamed that my baby would be the first to find fault
with my "mother's" body. So much for a child's infinite gratitude!

—⟊⟊—

As for the benefits of breastfeeding, I was immersed in my career as a journalist when I had both of my daughters. Among other duties, I regularly wrote a column on nutrition and spent much time advocating breastfeeding as the cheapest, safest and best food for children from birth to three months at least. I knew that breastfeeding safeguards against infection, prevents tooth decay in later life, has numerous nutrients that cannot be artificially reproduced in any formula, assists in normal growth and development of the child and helps the mother's healing and recovery. All of this is supported by the American Academy of Pediatrics, which advocates breast milk as "the preferred feeding for all infants, including premature and sick newborns, with rare exceptions." The academy further recommends that babies are breastfed exclusively for six months and continue up to a year after solid foods are introduced, or for long as the mother and child finds it desirable.

This position is derived from the abundance of scientific data showing that breast milk decreases the incidence and severity of diarrhea, lower-respiratory infections, ear infections, blood infection, bacteremia, bacterial meningitis, botulism, urinary tract infection, and necrotizing enterocolitis (an inflammatory bowel disease).[4] Breastfeeding is also thought to provide protection against Sudden Infant Death Syndrome (SIDS), insulin-dependent diabetes, Crohn's disease, ulcerative colitis, lymphoma and other chronic digestive diseases. Some researchers even believe that it enhances cognitive development in young children.

Besides the fact that some blood-borne viruses, such as hepatitis B or HIV, can be passed on through breast milk, there are no known disadvantages to breastfeeding the young child. Objections to breastfeeding, where they exist, are purely social, stemming partly from the perception of the breasts as objects of sexual desire rather than the mammary gland—the built-in mechanism for women to nurture their young, as cows, dogs and other mammals do.

For me, breastfeeding my daughters was my only choice—a fundamental one that my nine-year-old was now rejecting out of pity for me. That she was doing it meant little to me in any concrete way since, if I had to do it all over again, I would make the very same choice. The lesson that I took away from her comments, therefore, was far more general: like how hard we try, as mothers, to do what *we* think is best for our children, even at great costs to ourselves, and how quickly they will reject them as contrary to common sense and to their own value systems. Far beyond concerns about what my daughter thought of my body, her comment triggered a raging debate in my mind over just how responsible we are for and to our children, and how far we should go in the quest to give them better lives.

As mothers, we make great sacrifices, often not caring about ourselves and certain that they are best for our children. We sacrifice our own sense of well being—staying in a bad marriage or relationship, for example, just for the sake of the children. We sacrifice quality time with them in order to climb the career ladder or work two jobs to buy them all the *stuff* we think they need. We take on bigger mortgages than we can afford so that our children can grow up in the "right" house, in the "right" neighborhood and attend the "right" school. Rarely do we ever stop to ask them—the subjects of our obsessions—what they think, and rarer still do we ever stop to think and digest the fact that in many instances, if they were given the option, they would reject outright the choices we make for them.

I have never regretted breastfeeding my children at the cost of young perky breasts. But since that encounter with Ilsa, I am far more conscious of the fact that children do have minds of their own; that as they grow older, they have a right to choose their own destinies, irrespective of our plans for them. I realized too that Alya and Ilsa will make their own choices regardless of what I think; that I do not own their thoughts and they do not have to fit into my master plan for them.

It was around that time too that I began to pray for modest changes in my life—like enough money for a house with two bathrooms.

FIVE

Wholly Mother

Courage is not the absence of fear, but rather the judgment that something is more important than fear.

—Ambrose Redmoon

Ilsa was plucked from the pool, coughing and sputtering, before I realized that she had been drowning right before my eyes.

It was the day before New Year's Eve, 1999. My sister, my cousin and his wife, and our combined four children, were lounging poolside at a dreamy little villa in Central Florida, a few miles up the road from Disney World.

It was around fifty degrees outside, much warmer than what we left behind in Maryland.

I am island born. Cold, gray days smacking of melancholy run counter to the warmth and vibrancy of my island soul. Always, a part of me longs for sunshine and warm tropical days. It is a thirst, a craving brought on by dreariness of any kind and one that only sunshine can fill. Winters on the East Coast are often quite difficult therefore. Thus, my cousin's invitation to join him and his family in Florida while they visited from London was a godsend. The beautiful villa with the heated indoor pool where we stayed was a luxury I could never afford on my own. We cranked up the heat inside, and surrounded by tropical shades of azure and aquamarine, I fooled myself that we were in luxuriantly green Port Antonio on Jamaica's north east coast.

My children were in the pool with their two British cousins. The cousins' father, Andrew, and I sat next to each other on matching peach-and-green-striped chaise lounges. Next to us was his wife, Susan, and my sister, Lor.

Andrew was born and raised in London, the second child of an uncle with whom I had a love-hate relationship from the first time I met him when I was ten years old until his death more than twenty years later. His death, in 1992, brought his son to Jamaica for the first time and somehow through the melee of a big funeral service and extended relatives, we picked each other out as friends. In the ensuing years, we kept in touch as best as we could, a phone call here and there or a postcard or two. Seven years later, we were together again, celebrating the penultimate year of the twentieth century and the beginning of the twenty-first.

Since we had last seen each other, we had both added a daughter to our families. Now, the four children were in the pool, thrashing about with a green life-size rubber alligator. We watched from the poolside and chatted about the double-edged nature of life in the Caribbean vis-à-vis life in the United States and Great Britain for people of color.

Andrew had a unique perspective; he is black but a Briton by birth, raised by his West Indian parents in London. Now married to a white woman, he is father of two biracial children. Although he never set foot on Jamaica until he was thirty-seven years old, he felt an immediate affinity to the place and the people, he said. Suddenly he had a frame of reference for what it meant to belong somewhere and it was not England.

"Let's face it," he said, "there is no such thing as a black Englishman. I mean, they tolerate me, but they know I don't belong there and I know that I don't either." He paused. "Would you go back home—to Jamaica, I mean?"

My answer hung on the air. On the split screen of my life, I saw myself standing in Jamaica where the sun shines brighter than any other place on earth. I saw myself running barefooted in the streets, the way I used to as a child. I heard the sounds of children's laughter spilling from everywhere like pure, clean water. I heard the irresistible beat of reggae music—struggle songs—thumping out from giant boxes on street corners in the cities. I saw, felt, *knew* the *joi de vivre of* Jamaican culture, so often unfathomable alongside the crushing poverty that was everywhere. I contemplated the ardor of transforming that life into something meaningful. It could take a lifetime.

On the other side, I saw my life in the tiny but tidy two-bedroom apartment I shared with my daughters in Maryland. Life there was mundane and predictable. It was structured to a tee and personally autonomous as long as I could pay my bills. So often, I feared that I might not be able to. It is for me one of the greatest fears as a transplant in America because the inability to support myself would not just mean the loss of home and hearth; it would mean the loss of my dignity as a human being.

But this was America. For the most part, the bus system worked, the schools were good and the neighborhoods safe. Alya and Ilsa qualified for free breakfast and free lunch at school since my graduate assistant's stipend put me way below the poverty line. They qualified as well for free basic health and dental care from Montgomery County, I found out after much angst.

And, there is something called the American Dream. It is alive and well just outside the window, like a beautiful fairy dancing on a brisk wind. It is there for me—for everyone who could reach out and grasp it. I had to try. It was my only hope for a better way for my daughters and me, and it was why I had made the difficult choice to trade in Jamaica's *joi de vivre* for my structured life in Maryland.

I swallowed my spit and prepared to answer.

Andrew shot up from the chaise, cutting off my thoughts. In a few quick strides he was on the other side of the pool bending over, reaching low for Ilsa, calling her name with gentle urgency. Sputtering and coughing, she grabbed the hand he dipped into the pool. He hauled her out, her bright orange bathing suit clinging to her tiny body. Her rib cage contracted, expanded and contracted again as she took in great big gulps of air.

I kicked over my glass of lemonade on my way to the other side of the pool.

"What's wrong? What...? What's wrong?"

The words struggled to come out of my mouth.

"She had the alligator on top of her. She was trying to get from under it and she couldn't."

"She was drowning?"

"Ahh.... She could have."

"But I didn't notice. I didn't see anything..."

"I saw her. She was struggling..." he said.

"She was *drowning*?" I asked again.

"It's okay," he said gently. "She will be fine."

No, I told myself. It was not okay. I should have been watching her far more carefully than I thought I had been. I was only a few feet away from the pool's edge, near enough to get my feet wet from the splashing water.

She was an emerging swimmer with far more spunk than skill—just the type that needed eagle-eyed attention. But my mind had wandered. I had become far more interested in the conversation with Andrew than I was in what I thought was benign play in the pool, among four cousins of nearly the same age.

This was a major failing. As her mother, I have a responsibility to keep her safe, and until she reached a certain age at least, to put her needs above my own. Although fathers have their special roles to play in their children's lives, it is the mother, the female of the species, to whom nature entrusts the sacred responsibility of nurturing the young from conception to birth. Implicit in this relationship, is a bond as deep and as eternal as life itself and a sense of duty like no other. Mothers must not fail—cannot afford to because usually when they do, it spells disaster for the children and in many cases, the entire family structure.

This bond between women and their children funnels a special mother instinct that ensures she is deeply tuned in to her children's needs. She is committed to their well-being in a way that she cannot help. It is fuelled by a duty, a desire, a love that is inimitable and unchained. It powers the antennae that signals choking, under-feeding, overfeeding, infectious diseases, fires, accidents, drowning or anything else that might threaten their offspring.

Mothers devote their time to the physical, social and emotional well-being of their children even when they are busy around the house, washing, cleaning and cooking, trying to ensure an attractive, pleasant and healthy environment. As if that were not enough, modern society dictates that more and more women are in the workforce, sometime in search of personal fulfillment, but more often because they must contribute to their household incomes. In many instances, particularly in the African-American community, mothers are the sole providers.

Different societies have devised unique ways to recognize the multifaceted roles of women and mothers. The early Greeks celebrated Rhea, Mother of the Gods, with fine food, drinks and flowers at dawn, in the spring of each year; the Romans built a temple to honor their Magna Mater or Great Mother, Mother of All Gods, whom they seek to please with fine gifts at the Festival of Hilaria, held in March of each year; and in the early 17th century, England designated the fourth Sunday during the Lenten season as "Mothering Sunday."

Today, in keeping with a U.S. tradition that began in the early 20th century, most of the world celebrates Mother's Day on the second Sunday in May. The day is defined by tremendous commercialism, and merchants—perhaps more so than mothers—are the greatest beneficiaries. This contrasts sharply with the intent of Julia Ward Howe, a Boston activist and author of the *Battle Hymn of the Republic*, who first conceptualized a special day to honor the work of mothers. Concerned about the impact on her generation of the American Civil war and the Franco-Prussian War, Howe, in 1870, proposed a Mother's Day of Peace; she believed that women bore the brunt of wars with the loss of their husbands and sons.

"Why," she pleaded, "do not the mothers of mankind interfere in these matters to prevent the waste of that human life of which they alone bear and know the cost?"[5]

Howe's version of "mother's day" did not quite catch on, but Anna Jarvis's did. A Pennsylvania native, she wanted to honor the memory of her mother, Ann Marie Reeves Jarvis who, in the 1850s, organized Mother's

Friendship Clubs to fight the poor social conditions that she blamed for the lost of eight of her twelve children, all before they reached age seven.

When the American Civil War began, the elder Jarvis asked her clubs to pledge that the war would not impact their friendships, regardless of which side of the conflict they supported. Ultimately, the members of the club also nursed and saved the lives of many Union and Confederate soldiers. When the war was over, the elder Jarvis continued her efforts to unite families and communities and in 1868, organized a Mother's Friendship Day, "to revive the dormant filial love and gratitude we owe to those who gave us birth. To be a home tie for the absent. To obliterate family estrangement. To make us better children by getting us closer to the hearts of our good mothers. To brighten the lives of good mothers. To have them know we appreciate them, though we do not show it as often as we ought...Mothers Day is to remind us of our duty before it is too late."[6]

When Ann Marie died in 1905, Anna Jarvis sought to make true her mother's expressed wish that someone, sometime, will found a Memorial Mother's Day commemorating her for the matchless service she renders to humanity in every field of life.

In 1907, Anna Jarvis held a gathering at her home to commemorate her mother's life. A year later, she persuaded her mother's old church in Grafton, West Virginia, to celebrate Mother's Day on the second Sunday in May, the anniversary of her mother's death. By 1911, Mother's Day was celebrated in most of the United States and in 1914, President Woodrow Wilson officially designated the second Sunday of May each year as Mother's Day. It soon caught on in the rest of the world. Mother's Day, as it was originally conceived by Jarvis, captured the essence of women's lives and the challenges implicit in the multiple roles they play.

I understand these challenges as most women do. I also understand the desire for perfection and the instinctive need to create harmonious homes, serene communities and a world in which peaceful coexistence is possible. All of this translates into safety and the protection of our children from senseless wars, unconscionable predators, drunk drivers and accidents such as drowning. Most importantly, I understand the feeling of failure when we are forced to accept that our best was not good enough. Ilsa's near-accident in the pool was one of those days for me.

She was ready to get back in long before I fully digested what had almost happened.

I hugged her to me.

"Give it a break, Ilsa. You need to rest."

"But Mommy I want to go back! I was having fun!"

I let her go.

It was either that or condemn her to live forever in the shadows of my fears.

I watched her grab the alligator float by its snout on her way back in and I paused to write myself a few quick notes: First, plastic alligators in indoors pools can be just as deadly as real ones lurking under the cover of marsh, muck and swamp so always pay attention. Second, being physically present does not mean the same thing as paying attention or being available. Third, the known way is at times as treacherous as the unknown. Finally, mothers—women—as much as we are sometimes tempted to believe we are infallible, we are only humans and by that definition, bound to make mistakes. The trick to successful parenting is to try hard to minimize the mistakes, but when they do happen, grab the alligator by the snout and jump right back in without fear or recrimination.

SIX

Thou Shalt Not Kill

One step must start each journey, one word must start a prayer, one heart can know what is true, one life can make a difference.

—Author Unknown

"**H**ow would you like it if someone killed you, plucked your feathers and stuffed you in a blazing hot oven?"

It was a typical Sunday in our house. My aim was to cook a perfectly roasted chicken to go along with the inevitable rice and red beans; Alya's was to get me to abandon the project. Her concern for the members of the animal kingdom which began early in her life, was fermenting into a deep, well-thought out philosophy of non-violence against man and beast. She figured her campaign should begin in her own house, even though my chickens came to it already dead and frozen.

I was a carnivore, like most of the world. I grew up that way and for a long time never really questioned it, even though my Seventh Day Adventist background emphasized, without stipulating, vegetarianism. While, I accepted that it was a healthier lifestyle, I saw it as something akin to being left-handed in a right-handed world or going to Church on Saturdays instead of Sundays. It was against the tide—an inconvenience—and therefore, a more difficult goal to reach.

So, I continued to eat poultry and fish but generally shunned red meat. It was not that difficult since I never cared for beef and worst, pork, which my religion forbids. The only meat I missed was the spicy curried goat on white rice I loved to eat in Jamaica.

Alya, meanwhile, was growing increasingly uncomfortable with any kind of animal protein—except the dried salted fish, another Jamaican favorite, especially when combined with ackee, our national fruit. As I watched her struggle, it became clear to me that she could not separate the dead meat on her plate from the animal life around her—the neighbors' cats and dogs, the frisky deer in the nearby woods, the geese and ducks in the parks and the fish in the giant aquarium at Han Ah Reum, the Asian supermarket at Georgia and Shorefield.

She seemed especially rattled by the sight of a whole chicken going into the oven. Thus began her march behind me every time I tried to roast one.

"How would you like it if someone killed you, plucked your feathers and stuffed you in an oven?" she asked angrily.

"I am not a bird and I don't have feathers," I retorted.

My response was lighthearted at first, but over time, I grew weary of Alya's interrogations. I still did not see anything wrong with eating a piece of chicken now and then, especially as I was not actually killing the fowl myself, but Alya would not let me forget that someone had to kill it before it made it into my oven. Eventually, she gave up eating meat completely except for fresh fish—as long as she did not see it alive first.

"I have a problem with it Mommy," she explained one day as we shopped at Han Ah Reum. "One minute the fish is running around looking at me and the next minute it's on my plate. I just can't eat it."

I knew what she meant—sort of. As a child, my father kept a tiny herd of goats. It was our biggest investment, a buffer against hard times out of the ordinary, such as sickness or death, or for special occasions like Christmas or a wedding. In those times, we would kill the goats and eat the meat ourselves if we had nothing else; kill them and sell most of it and keep the leftovers, or sell a whole goat or two depending on what was needed. Eventually, we found that no matter how hard times got, none of us could eat the meat from the goats we raised from the time they were kids until they were fully grown. Not the ones we named Wendy, Miss Gift, Jenny, Flash, Billy, Claudette, Brownie—or countless others—and nurtured just like we did the little boys and girls in the family. Selling the goats became just as traumatic with each child refusing to part with the goats in the herd for which he or she had special responsibility. My father mostly gave up raising the goats, tacitly acknowledging that the few we had were pets like the dogs.

My belief in vegetarianism as a healthier and more positive approach to human relationships with other living things naturally made me sympathetic to Alya's choice. I was determined to support her even if I was not quite ready to convert. Of course, this complicated my life some more as I now had to prepare different meals on limited time and an even more limited budget.

Alya struggled with being a vegetarian too. Her first attempt, at age eleven, lasted a month. At fourteen, she tried again and for more than three years remained resolute in her practice of lacto-ovo-pesco vegetarianism. This means that her protein needs are satisfied primarily by eating fish and shellfish and sparse amounts of eggs, cheese and milk.

Nutritionists say this is actually a very good diet for a teenager, particularly because vegetarians tend to include more fruits and vegetables than normal in their diet. My daughter's choice to continue to eat fish and some dairy products ensures that she is getting an adequate supply of nutrients such as iron, protein, zinc, calcium and Vitamins D and B12, all necessary for healthy growth and organ function.

Alya's conversion to vegetarianism and her discipline in following it through have been both enlightening and reassuring for me. Often enough, I had worried that my firstborn seemed a little too self-indulgent—that she did not have the discipline to do something so difficult. Secretly, I worried too about her interests in trends and fads. Rather than seeing them for what they were—the evolution of a typical teenager growing up in America—I worried that they might be indicative of character traits that I found unappealing. As she grew older and began to assert herself, I knew that once again, I had worried without cause. Her resolve dispelled any doubts I had and increased my respect for her. More than that, it inspired me to do much better for myself and my own health. I began to research the benefits of a vegetarian diet and to actively pursue it as my preferred way of life.

Along the way, I discovered that some of the world's most revered philosophers were vegetarians. For example, Pythagoras, the mathematician, argued that:

As long as man continues to be the ruthless destroyer of lower living beings, he will never know health or peace. For as long as men massacre animals, they will kill each other. Indeed, he who sows the seeds of murder and pain cannot reap joy and love.

Leo Tolstoy believed that by killing animals for food, humankind suppresses its own and highest spiritual capacity—that of sympathy and pity toward living creatures like himself—and instead learns to be cruel. He asked:

While our bodies are the living graves of murdered animals, how can we expect any ideal conditions on earth?

Leonardo Da Vinci, Socrates, Plato, Clement of Alexandria, Plutarch, King Ashoka, Montaigne, Akbar the Great, John Milton, Sir Isaac Newton, Voltaire, Percy Bysshe Shelley, Ralph Waldo Emerson, Henry David Thoreau, George Bernard Shaw, Hans Christian Andersen, Louisa May Alcott, Mahatma Gandhi and Albert Einstein, were all vegetarians.[7]

Like many of these deep thinkers, Alya's embrace of vegetarianism reflected a quest for a deeper understanding of the human condition. It started deep inside her heart—inside her search for a better way of being.

Interestingly enough, this was the major goal of the founders of the British Vegetarian Society in 1842. Rather than being purely concerned with a diet that did not include meat, they were interested in vegetarianism as a means to a higher end. In fact, the word "vegetarian," which was coined by the society, has its origin in the Latin word "vegetus" meaning "whole, sound, fresh or lively." This suggests the interconnectedness between human beings with the wholeness of life—our relationship with other living things.

While Christianity in general does not advocate vegetarianism, subgroups, such as the Seventh Day Adventists, have always promoted it as a purer and healthier lifestyle. Other religions such as Rastafarianism, Hinduism and Buddhism also advocate vegetarianism. Outside of religious or philosophical considerations, many contemporary medical experts are certain of the benefits of a balanced vegetarian diet. Indeed, research suggests that vegetarianism correlates strongly with reduced risk of chronic conditions, such as heart disease, obesity, type II diabetes, hypertension and some types of cancer. The American Dietetics Association says that a well-planned vegetarian diet is beneficial in the prevention and treatment of certain diseases and decreases the mortality rate among sufferers.

As my commitment to greater wholeness and a more balanced life intensifies, I am humbled and intrigued by the thought that even though I had flirted with this tradition for more than two decades, even though I was heavily influenced by religious practices and by significant health concerns, in the end, it was my young child, who, by her example, showed me that I could do it.

Still, the challenges are far from over. My younger daughter, Ilsa, loves a good steak. Her attitude toward meat eating is based on her philosophy that: "If God did not want us to eat animals, he should not have made their meat so tasty!"

I will be preparing different meals for a good while yet.

SEVEN

No More Tears

We shall find peace. We shall hear angels.
We shall see the sky sparkling with diamonds.

—Anton Pavlovich Chekhov

"How will I know my parents when I get to heaven?"

I paused halfway in my effort to pull the clothes out of the washer. It was in the middle of such a mundane task that Ilsa asked me a question to which I had no real answer.

No mother is ever truly prepared for the questions their children ask, especially ones that so profoundly speak to the nature of our lives on earth and its greatest certainty—that it is temporary and what comes after is the great mystery of our existence. So, right away I began musing: now that I think of it, how will I know my children when I get to heaven?

Momentarily, I am saddened by the thoughts triggered by the question—thoughts that I could not escape in my attempt to frame an answer; thoughts of death and dying; of my own mortality, amplified by the relentless passing of the years; of eternal separation from the ones I love; of Christianity and some of its fundamental complexities, contradictions even.

As Christians, we believe in heaven, for example. We believe that it is paradise, even if the nature of it remains fuzzy and undefined, but few of us are ever in any real hurry to get there. In the same vein, we accept the inevitably of death, the door that we must pass through *en route*, yet most of us never truly embrace it. Instead, we resist it with everything we have. We resist because, our faith notwithstanding, we fear the irrevocable entry into the great unknown. We resist because we loathe the thought of eternal separation from the ones we love. We resist because we still have places to go, people to see, desires to satisfy and dreams to fulfill. We resist because life, as anguished as it can be sometimes, is mostly wonderful.

Few among us, even those of us who have known more than our fair share of pain, would deny ourselves the opportunity to walk this earth, to experience the rain and the sunshine on our faces; to feel fine powdery sand filtering through our fingers or toes; to stand and contemplate the mysterious, magical grandeur of the ocean and skies; to meet the people whom we have met; to love those whom we have loved and be loved by those who have loved us; to be among the host of people, animals and spirits traversing together on this great journey called life. This is why it is so hard to contemplate leaving, even for the promise of a bigger, greater paradise.

I turned the question over in my mind and pondered how frightening eternity would be without my girls. As well, I pondered the core presumption—that there is in fact a heaven and a God, and that we will be among those who will find our way there when our lives on earth comes to an end.

I went to Sunday School and Sabbath School as a child. Then, I accepted without even thinking about it that there was a God. I believed this God was the Master of the Universe and he lived in heaven, a place of incomparable beauty, beyond the clouds. This heaven would be the final destination for all who served God during their lives on earth.

As an adult, I have not gone to church as much. Still, I embrace the idea of a living God, and I have taught the children as much. In my struggles to be who I think God wants me to be, I shun excessive commercialism, especially of religious holidays. Easter, for example, has nothing to do with bunnies or eggs; it is about the death and resurrection of The Christ. Nor is Christmas about Santa Claus; it is about the birth of Jesus and the hope for redemption for the sins of mankind.

We pray. We read our Bibles. We attend church on those occasions when we do not allow our lives to get in the way.

Now, I no longer believe, as I did as a child, that God is a white man with blue eyes, clothed in flowing white robes, sitting on a golden throne. Indeed, I have no concept of what he looks like, but in my moments of pique at both sexism and racism, I have happily conceptualized God as a black woman with dreadlocks just like Whoopi Goldberg. And, I have imagined the look on the face of Pat Robertson, and others like him, when he stands before her and recognize that *this* indeed is God.

God, I now believe, is less of a physical being and more of a presence, an overwhelming force that is the origin and arbiter of goodness and grace. This force is the very essence of the ideals of equality, justice, peace, faith, love, kindness, gentleness and everything that is pure and good in life.

While my concept of God has evolved, my belief in his existence and his status as Supreme Lord and Master of the Universe has never wavered. Although I understand the evolution theory, for example, as the scientific explanation of how the earth came into being, I accept the creation story as an act of faith. It is a faith that is validated every time I hear a newborn baby cry; see the magnificence of a sunrise or a sunset; stand on the sand and contemplate the depth and vastness of the ocean; hear the songs of the birds in my backyard; or consider the perfection and harmony of the universe. Such beauty and correctness could only have come, not by chance, but from the mind of a being far superior to any other, far more loving, far more compassionate and with a sense of humor that knows no end.

I believe deeply in God, even if it means that I live in a fool's paradise; even if it's just a way to numb the pain of my existence sometimes; even if such faith is merely the "opium of the oppressed;"[8] even if it's escapism; even if it's a crutch; even if it all sounds like a magnificent lie at times; even if there are more questions than answers;

even if it's just a way to make sense of a journey that seems pointless at times. This, I know, is blind faith but on this one issue only, I am happy to be completely blind.

—⁓—

Implicit in the question—how will I know my parents when I get to heaven?—is my daughter's acceptance that our lives on earth are temporary as well as her trust in what I have taught her and the extent to which I have influenced her belief. I am humbled and deeply touched by her simple faith.

"I would know you anywhere," I said suddenly, thinking about her wonderful strength of character, the force of her personality and the surety of purpose that has defined her from birth. "My spirit will know your beautiful spirit even among a host of angels."

Instinctively, she seemed to know that there was not much I could give to her—that it was a much bigger question than I could answer—but whatever I could, would be enough.

"Okay," she said, the beginning of a happy smile already in her voice. I dug deeper for a little more.

"Heaven is such a perfect place," I added, remembering the words of St. John in the book of Revelation:

And I saw a new heaven and a new earth: for the first heaven and the first earth were passed away... And God shall wipe away all tears from their eyes: and there shall be no more death, neither sorrow, nor crying, neither shall there be any more pain for the former things are passed away.[9]

And the Apostle Paul in his letter to the Corinthians:

Behold, I show you a mystery; We shall not all sleep, but we shall all be changed. In a moment, in the twinkling of an eye, at the last trump: for the trumpet shall sound, and the dead shall be raised incorruptible, and we shall be changed. For this corruptible must put on incorruption and this mortal must put on immortality…then shall be brought to pass the saying that is written, Death is swallowed up in victory.[10]

"I am not sure how it will work, but I know that, there, we will have nothing to worry about. You see, God has it all worked out. So, I am pretty sure that all the babies will know which angels are their mommies, and all the mommies will know which little angels are their babies."

She smiled radiantly and wandered off, back to the television in the family room.

I resumed unloading the washer, picking up socks and tee shirts one at a time. The mindless task left my brain free to think of the pathway to heaven, of the door that must be unlocked at the end of the journey before its great mysteries are revealed. Free to ponder a baffling question: How will I know my children when I get to heaven?

EIGHT

Living Truth

*Your children will see what you're all about by what you live
rather than what you say*

—Wayne Dyer

"So are we going to do it?" my cousin Andrew asked his wife,
waving what looked like a thick white sock. Her response
was unintelligible.

I watched them from the breakfast table while I sucked on my
orange and our children exchanged little packs of Cheerios for Froot
Loops and Apple Jacks among themselves, until each had the cereal he
or she wanted.

It was New Year's Eve, 1999. We were on our Orlando trip,
preparing to spend the day at Disney World for the big end of the
'90s celebrations. We arrived by train the day before, through Central
Florida's magnificent terrain—an endless vista of orange trees laden
with yellow fruits, pausing only to make room for the countless lakes,
ponds, streams and gorges.

Andrew and his wife Susan were visiting from London and had
weeklong passes to Disney. We didn't. I had only enough for the grand
finale and planned to buy only a one-day pass to the Magic Kingdom
on New Year's Eve.

We did not miss anything as it turned out. The day before, on their first attempt, the cousins spent the entire day at the theme park without making a dent in the lines of patrons waiting to go on the rides. That experience accounted for the little plan they hatched, which was unfolding as we ate breakfast.

"Uh...Uh...are we going to do it?" Andrew asked again.

I looked at Susan. Her face was turning beet red all the way to the roots of her long blond hair.

"Ask your cousin," she muttered finally.

"Ask me what?" I queried, curious at the sudden unease in their demeanor.

"Well, you know," Andrew began. "Yesterday we only got on one of the rides, but we found out that wheelchair users and their entire party get to go to the head of the line. So, we thought if we faked it and use a wheelchair we could actually make a few more rides today."

Enlightenment dawned. The white thing Andrew had in his hand was a store-bought bandage slated for the foot of the prospective wheelchair user.

I didn't want to lecture my family. They were good people and slightly older than I was. Plus, this vacation together was an ongoing process of getting to know each other and building what I hoped would be lifelong friendships between us and our children. I appreciated too that they wanted to get something for their money before returning to London on New Year's Day. I truly understood the dilemma, but I didn't like the plan, harmless as it seemed.

Most of us know someone with a disability, even if from a distance. I am fortunate enough to not to have had firsthand experience but this certainly does not preclude an appreciation for the challenges that certain kinds of disability present. I recall too an experience at the University Hospital of the West Indies in Kingston when I gave birth to Ilsa, my second daughter. The rooms were semi-private with fabric screens rather than walls separating the beds in the recovery room. Through a sleepy veil, as I recovered from a cesarean birth and anesthesia, I still could process a conversation somewhere close to me—a doctor explaining to a new mother that her baby was not normal. Yes, she had ten fingers and ten toes, but she also had a genetic abnormality that would negatively affect her physical, intellectual and language development for the rest of her life. She had Down syndrome, a cognitive disorder caused by the presence of an extra chromosome. Individuals with this condition suffer mild to severe developmental disabilities. They are also characterized by some distinct physical traits such as a round face, small chin, slanted eyes and shorter limbs.

The doctor delivered the bad news kindly and left. The mother, who had listened quietly throughout, began to sob painfully. I drifted off to sleep again, my heart breaking for her and more grateful than ever that my little one was perfectly fine and sound asleep. What would I have felt, if I, not the mother next door, was the one on the receiving end of the bad news?

Down syndrome, however, is not the worst form of disability. Although most babies are born perfectly healthy and normal, a percentage of them, with varying disabilities, may never see the sun, hear birds singing or music playing; walk, run, play sports; or otherwise fulfill all the rich expectations most parents have for their newborns.

Then, there are disabilities that come about as a result of accidents—a slip in the bathtub, a dive at an awkward angle, an out-of-control car driven by a drunk driver—and in an instant, a life can be changed forever with anyone of us going from independent to dependent, from able-bodied to disabled.

Regardless of the cause or nature of their disability, those who find themselves afflicted are the likeliest to be excluded from the mainstream, sometimes out of prejudice and sometimes because many of us do not know how to relate to people who are different.

No, disability was no joke and it was nothing to call down on ourselves just so we could get to the front of the line at Disney. Moreover, the children were watching. I could never risk them thinking, even for a moment, that the situation was funny or that it was okay to participate in an act of deception. I could not, because as a teacher and a parent—or just a human being—I realized a long time ago that children live what they learn and further, that the easiest way to lead was by example. If I allowed them to see me lying, it would be so much harder to insist that they tell the truth. If I allowed them to see me cheating, it would be so much harder to insist on honesty from them. If I allowed them to see me participate in subterfuge, it would be so much harder to insist on sincerity and authenticity.

I held up my hand.

"No," I said. "Please don't let us do this."

"I should have known," Susan mumbled in her short clipped almost comical speaking tone. "There's no way someone who eats carrots and oranges for breakfast would agree to anything like this!"

"But Grace, you could use the chair. You weren't feeling well yesterday. You are not supposed to overexert yourself," Andrew said, trying to volunteer my foot for the bandage he had bought to legitimize the wheelchair, and to quiet the voices in his head that was telling him that it was a cheap trick.

I balked.

"Oh no, not my foot. I will be fine, thank you very much."

They abandoned the plan, not merely because I objected, but because they were not entirely committed to it. After all, Andrew was Uncle Maurice's son and my uncle would have strung him up for even thinking about it.

It took us nearly two hours of slow crawling through a maze of traffic to make the short drive from the villa in Claremont to Disney World. We arrived and purchased our tickets minutes before sales closed for the day at 10 a.m. The Magic Kingdom was at capacity with just over six hundred thousand people already inside.

After that, the challenge was staying together—four adults and four children among a sea of bodies and a gaggle of languages from all over the world. That, though, was a part of the adrenaline rush—being one with this tidal wave of humanity in fantasyland, on the cusp of a new millennium.

We made it onto three rides only: Space Mountain, Splash Mountain and Buzz Lightyear's Space Ranger Spin. I skipped the first two. Space Mountain sounded fearsome and both it and Splash Mountain warned that thrill-seekers needed to be in good health, free from motion sickness, back or neck problems, heart problems or other conditions that could be aggravated by the ride. Since I was unsure how many of those conditions I had, I let the children go with the cousins. When it was over, they were certain I had made the right decision because Space Mountain was baaaaaddddddd!

I watched from the other side while they tumbled down Splash Mountain. After that, we all piloted our own star cruisers, spun through outer space and fired laser cannons on the Buzz Lightyear's Space Ranger. I let myself go in the seductive world of fantasy.

It was amazing.

Finally, we took the Big Thunder Railroad through Frontierland and later, soaked up the sights and sounds of Main Street USA. We walked by classic rides such as the "Haunted Mansion," "Teacups" and "Pirates of the Caribbean," all of which had lines more than a few days long. Realizing that ours was not the ultimate Disney experience, I promised the kids that we would return some other time.

They were happy, and I was too. Not only because on the eve of my birthday, Buzz Lightyear made me feel like a kid again, but because we had made it on a few rides without resorting to trickery, harmless as it might have appeared.

NINE

In His Own Image

To fling my arms wide
In some place of the sun,
To whirl and to dance
Till the white day is done.
Then rest at cool evening
Beneath a tall tree
While night comes on gently,
Dark like me—
That is my dream!

To fling my arms wide
In the face of the sun,
Dance! Whirl! Whirl!
Till the quick day is done.
Rest at pale evening...
A tall, slim tree...
Night coming tenderly
Black like me.

—Langston Hughes

"**W**hy did you make my skin so dark?"

Ilsa was in the first grade when she hurled the question at me. She had been in America for only a year and was newly conscious of her black skin, it seemed. Suddenly, she wasn't just feeling like something was wrong with her, she was blaming me for it.

My soul wept a little. No child should feel that anything about her—anything about the way God made her—made her less than anyone else. But, I am a black woman too, born and raised in a post-colonial culture where great significance is attached to skin color. And, long before I ever set foot on American soil, I knew of its history of racism, manifested in segregation and Jim Crow laws, that until a few decades ago, defined the preferred form of human interactions. Under the guise of "separate but equal," blacks were relegated to second class citizens in the land of their birth.

—⟋⟍—

April 4, 1968. I was three years and three months old. I was at home with Mama, my baby sister Hazel, and my cousin, Everton—Ever for short. Ever is three years older than I am at the most, so he would have been around six at the time. Since my sister, who follows me in birth order, was born on May 25, 1967 and would have been a little more than a month shy of her first birthday, I have to conclude she was inside the house with Mama on that fateful morning. I do not believe my father was at home, because he—the greatest politician who never was—would have been in the picture and I have no such recollection.

Ever was best friend to my older brother, Ian. In fact they were inseparable from those early years of their lives to their teenage years. For some reason, Ian went to school on April 4, but Ever did not. He had to settle for playing with me in the loose dirt between the stones in front of our little house. That was where we were when Mama burst out of the house in a state of deep distress. She wanted me to run an important errand: to tell Bro' Sam, my father's uncle and the beloved rogue of the family, that "dem kill Dr. Martin Luther King." Bro' Sam was doing road work about a half mile away and would not have heard the news that my mother had on our little red transistor radio.

As soon as she delivered the message, she changed her mind: I would forget, she said. She instructed Ever to be the messenger and me to accompany him. The day would live in infamy in our family not only because of the civil rights leader's death, but because of the message my cousin delivered: "Bro, Sam! Bro, Sam! Miss Mary say dem kill Dr. Martin Luther Sheep!"

Later, I heard my parents talk about Stokely Carmichael and the freedom fighters and I began to have a sense that life was not too good for black folks in America, where two of my father's sisters lived. By age twelve, I had found James Baldwin's *Go Tell it on the Mountain* and the *Fire Next Time* in the library, and read both of them; I read Harper Lee's *To Kill a Mockingbird* a little later. The *Autobiography of Miss Jane Pittman*, handed to me by my English Language teacher, Mrs. Barbara Walters, when I was about sixteen, drew my tears and my sorrow. It didn't matter that that particular work was fiction; it clearly had a basis in reality. After that, I pretty much understood what life had been like for black folks in America.

—⁓—

During slavery, Africans, kidnapped and brought to America, were not considered part of the human race. Rather, they were numbered among the animals on the estates. As their masters' property, not only did they perform backbreaking work on tobacco and sugar cane plantations, but they were also at his pleasure—to be disposed of, if and when they could no longer perform to his satisfaction. The end of slavery did not mean the end of inhumane treatment. Black oppression merely entered a new phase with laws designed to keep the races separate and Africans in their place—at the base of a stratified society.

It was somewhat different in Jamaica. Emancipation in 1838 meant a definite end to slavery. With many of the former slave masters headed back to England, newly freed Africans had a chance to begin a life free of the obstacles they faced as property on the plantations. Physical freedom, however, would not be enough to immediately dispense with psychological distortion. Many people aspired to replace the planters, understandably so since the top of the hierarchy is where great power and status reside. To truly replace "Buckra Massa," however, required one coveted, but humanly impossible attribute—whiteness. To that end, those who covet this quality hold in reverence others who, to varying degrees, had what they could not. Thus, people of lighter hue held pride of place in the society, a malady that remains prevalent today.

Otherwise, I am profoundly aware of a preponderance of attitudes in western culture that do not honor the humanity of non-white peoples—a reality that I wish my sweet little Ilsa would not have to confront.

Momentarily, my sadness was overtaken by dread at the thought that by moving to the United States, I had contributed to any sense of confusion on my child's part and that rather than growing up with a healthy self-concept and a sense of herself as the extraordinarily beautiful child of the universe that she is, she would end up loathing herself as so many people of African descent in the Western world seem to do. I thought of Pecola, in Tony Morrison's novel, *The Bluest Eye,* and her futile longing for attention—for the golden hair and blue eyes that she thought she needed—and how, when that attention came, it devastated her in ways she had not imagined. I thought too of Frantz Fanon's contention that:

> *A normal Negro child, having grown up within a normal family, will become abnormal on the slightest contact with the white world.*[11]

In Jamaica, Ilsa's contact with the "white world" was significantly limited. Further, she had the psychological advantage that came with being a member of the majority race and culture instead of the minority, which in some ways neutralizes the significance attached to skin color and ethnicity. What had I done, taking her from there to here? I groped to find clarity within the blankness my mind had become.

—ɯ—

Ilsa was six years old. Mercy, a Ghanaian who looked just like her, and Taylor, an American with pale yellow hair and gray-blue eyes, were her best friends. When Mercy moved away, tiny nymph-like Taylor became her best friend for a while. I observed their interactions, silently marveling at the bond between two little girls who, up until a year before, had never set eyes on each other. More than anything, I was relieved that having taken my girls from their native land, they seemed to be adjusting very well and experiencing, in some measure, the same kinds of deep friendship that I shared with my countless cousins and childhood friends in rural Jamaica.

Then she began to complain about her hair.

"Ouch! That hurts!"

Her protests became more exaggerated, no matter how gentle I was. I tried harder, determined that neither hot comb nor cold cream would touch her hair, especially since it was already quite thin. Someday, when she was older perhaps, I would consider it for ease of style—someday when I knew she had fully grasped that the sum total of who she was, the depth and breadth of her humanity, had nothing to do with the color of her skin, or the texture of her hair, or the shape of her nose. At that point, it would no longer matter how she wore her hair. Until then, she was my little girl and perfect just the way she was.

"Mommy, why did you make my skin so dark?"

We were walking toward the playground the day she stopped me in my tracks. I closed my eyes and contemplated my response. This was another moment when words needed to be chosen carefully and the answers sufficient to last a lifetime.

As I struggled to find the words to express what was in my heart, I imagined I heard the voice of my compatriot, Marcus Mosiah Garvey. His voice came as a magnificent boom.

"Tell her," he said. "Tell her that God made us as who we are. Tell her her skin had to be dark because she entered the world from betwixt the legs of a woman who came out of the cradle of human civilization, Mother Africa. Tell her that despite slavery and racism in the world, there is honor and dignity in being an African, for Africans too are children of God. Tell her to be strong in the face of an often-ignorant world that will sometimes try to equate her worth as a person with the color of her skin and try to diminish her because of it."

"You must tell her," Garvey said, "that the darkness of her skin only means the presence of all light and her duty and responsibility is to go forth into the world and let that light shine."

Then came the voice of Bob Marley, spoken to the low strum of his guitar. It was honeyed, confident and comforting.

"Yea," he said. "Tell the child(ren) the truth. And, tell her, none but ourselves can free our minds."

I tried to tell the truth so a six-year-old could understand—to give her an answer that then and in the years to come, would help to steer her clearly, firmly and decisively away from the confused abyss of self-hatred.

"First of all," I began slowly. "I did not make you even though you came through my body. God did, and he wanted your skin dark and beautiful just like mine. Don't you like Mommy's dark skin?"

"Ye-eh-es," she drawled thoughtfully.

"Well, yours is just like mine, and there is nothing wrong with it. In fact it is quite lovely. I have never seen anyone with skin as strong and rich and beautiful as yours. I really couldn't have made it either black or white, but if I could, I would have made it just as it is—just like mine because that way you could look like my baby just the way you do now. I love your skin baby, and I know you do too."

"I do love my skin mommy, but sometimes I wonder how come daddy is yellow and Alya is yellow, and sometimes I think white skin is better. Sometimes I want my skin to be like Taylor's... And yesterday there was a boy on the playground. He was calling me ugly...and darky and names like that." .

I plopped down on a fallen tree nearby and pulled her unto my lap. I breathed in deeply and exhaled again and again.

"Let's get a few things straight here," I said. "First, there is something profoundly wrong with anyone who thinks that something is wrong with you because your skin is dark. Apart from the fact that you are lovely inside and out, you have no control over what skin you would enter the world in. Blaming or hating someone for something they cannot control is ignorant and stupid. Second, white skin or light skin is not better. It's just different. Don't ever confuse difference with better. Do you understand?"

"Ye-eh-es."

"I am happy that you do, Baby. For as ignorant as it is, you are probably going to meet other people in your lifetime who will not like you just because your skin is dark. But you are going to have to learn to forgive their ignorance. Do you remember in Jamaica we say that when you see a duppy you should make the sign of the cross?"

"I don't think so. What does it mean?"

"Well, you know duppies are dead people, right? They belong in the spirit world and shouldn't be walking among the living. Some people think, though, that they sometimes get confused and come back to walk among us, and when that happens, we have to find a way to get them to scurry back in the other world where they belong. Most people believe that if you make the sign of the cross—like this—it will do it because the cross represents the power of Christ and it's enough to make ghosts run away.

"Well, it's the same way when you are confronted with ignorance. You are going to have to scare it away and you have to do that with the power of your soul. And, that is your beauty, your intelligence, your goodness and your confidence in who you are. You understand?"

I spoke earnestly, conscious that to some extent, she was merely responding to her new surroundings and that around her new friends, she was becoming more cognizant of the real issues that black women face —like our hair and what to do with it. Still, I was mindful that she too was responding to a composite of attitudes that not only define an ideal of beauty in ways that are non-black, but also reject the notion of blackness generally. The Western worldview, anchored in Christianity and Eurocentricity, for example, promotes fear of blackness as a construct—Satan, the Prince of Darkness, black magic, black sheep, black Fridays, black market, blackmail, black cats, black people—all inherently bad.

Although I have always been comfortable in my skin and with my place in the world, I have never been oblivious of the issues around skin color. Indeed, I could not have been, growing up in Jamaica, where skin color, since slavery, has so closely correlated with social class and status. In truth, after emancipation, color and social class largely became a function of each other with white and light-skinned people having more status and more opportunity for social mobility, while blacks languished in disproportionately large numbers at the bottom of the hierarchy.

If you black, stand back; if you brown stick around; if you white, you alright.

The oft used expression aptly captures the relationship between one's skin color and one's chances in life. Change has been slow in coming.

Against this background, my challenge as a parent was to raise my daughters to be human beings first, and to see their dark skin for what it is—a natural and unquestionable part of that humanity. Ilsa's question was a timely reminder that our children, at a very young age, become keenly aware of the premium that society places on race and skin color. Bombarded as they are by media images and real-life attitudes that define the ideal in ways that are non-black, it isn't difficult to process the message that, if white or whiteness is it, the farther away one happens to be from it, the less acceptable one will be. Long before my daughter's question, I knew I had a responsibility to help her understand the value of her humanity, separate and apart from variables like gender and race that society places so much emphasis on. After her question, I knew only that I had to try harder.

Ilsa is now a teenager. She is a kick-ass kind of gal who does not think for a single moment that the universe is not hers for the taking. She calls herself an enigma—the black child of an immigrant single mother, a gifted and talented student who loves horses, plays the piano, speaks and is fascinated by all things French, cares about the environment, and aspires to see the whole world.

She runs, jumps, skips, bulldozes, thinks her way through life without a care about color—hers or anyone else's. Just know that if you are in her way, she is going over you, under you, around you, through you. She is the epitome of regality, strength and dignity—an amazing child of the universe, an inimitable and indomitable spirit, a lovely and infinitely delightful citizen of the world.

TEN

The Chair In The White House

Only as high as I reach can I grow
Only as far as I seek can I go
Only as deep as I look can I see
Only as much as I dream can I be

—Karen Raven

Inside 1600 Pennsylvania Avenue, I let sink in the fact that I was actually there, walking where most of America's presidents have walked. Our tour led us to the Cabinet Room where I took special note of the President's chair. It was at the head of the table and about two inches or so taller than the others. Just to punctuate the moment, I pulled out the chair, sat and crossed my legs for just a few lingering moments.

It was July 4, 1999—two years before the horrors of September 11, 2001. The Secret Service agents looked on benignly from the hallway as the girls took their turns sitting in the chair. Later, in the blazing sun, we wandered out to the south lawn where we would meet President William Jefferson Clinton. I looked him in the eye and lingered just a little on his handshake.

His eyes are the color of the sea off Montego Bay on a sunny day—startlingly blue. The crow's feet, so visible on television, were nearly nonexistent in reality. He is ruggedly handsome, looking more like a slightly aging movie star than the astute politician and America's chief executive officer. I promptly added him to my list of handsome white guys. So far, it had only one on it—Tom Selleck.

At my feet, the children waited patiently. He bent low to shake their hands.

He is too warm, too engaging, too human to be overwhelming, but William Jefferson Clinton, the forty-second president of the United States, was no less distinguished, no less a force in the world than any previous resident of The White House. Moreover, his foibles notwithstanding, he was a favorite among people all over the world.

Child, how did you get here?

The question was a constant refrain in my mind. It happened every time I found myself in situations that were so far away from the realities I had known, that any comparison would be incongruous. It happened each time I sat on Metro's Red Line train heading toward Washington, D.C., gazing through the windows at the Washington Monument.

We had been on the Mall before—cherry-blossom gazing, touring the monuments, reveling in the rich sense of history and idealism that are so distinctly and proudly American. The Jefferson Memorial, dedicated to Thomas Jefferson, third president of the United States and avid political philosopher, was especially attractive to me. Many of his ideas on the rights of man, governments derived from the people, religious freedoms, the separation of church and state and equality of educational opportunities, are embossed in stone panels throughout and provide wonderful food for thought in a world where societies, including the United States, continue to struggle toward a common meeting place that sufficiently accommodates most, if not all, of those ideals.

Still, there is something about the Washington Monument— something about its loftiness that keeps my eyes going back, following its apex skyward. In its solidity, it is to me a proud symbol of America's strength and its enduring promise of a great community, albeit one that is still evolving. It symbolizes as well my own aspirations—to reach the very pinnacle of my dreams—and a longing for a more prosperous, stable and secure world—particularly in the Caribbean and Africa, the lands of my ancestors, where conflict and poverty, not real progress, are often the only constants. That world is necessary if my children's peers, the next generation, are to realize their full potential.

It's a long way from Sunday school to Broadway.

I heard the lines somewhere eons ago, but it meandered through my mind as I put my hand in President Clinton's at the White House on America's Independence Day.

It's a long way from nowhere to the corridors of power in the world, I paraphrased.

It was my second trip to the White House with Alya and Ilsa. How improbable! Yet, it was all too real down to the President in blue jeans and navy polo shirt.

It took me a while to realize that the prim and often absurd elitism of my post-colonial heritage was generally absent from public life in America. Conceivably, I could have gotten tickets to the White House tours on my own, as long as I was prepared to stand in line over a long period whenever they were being dispensed. But I was fortunate enough to know Omarosa Manigault, then scheduling correspondent for Vice President Al Gore. When she tendered the invitations, I happily accepted.

—◊—

Our first trip in December 1998 was surreal. It was a conversion of memories, of childhood wonder, of journalistic curiosity; of a mature, intellectual appreciation for the political symbol the White House represents as well as the history and cultural significance of the 18th century Georgian mansion.

The chair in the White House will rock no more.
The chair in the White House will rock no more.

I was a child, no more than four years old, and living in a remote village in rural Jamaica. For some reason, my mother, a woman with only an elementary-level education, kept repeating the phrase. It was my first recollection of a place thus named, and I soon began to realize it was somehow connected to a man who once lived there—John Fitzgerald Kennedy.

In time, the phrase began to make sense to me. Young, charming John F. Kennedy, the thirty-fifth president of the United States, and one of its most beloved, was assassinated before he could complete his first term in office. He was the revolutionary of his day— an Irish Catholic, deeply concerned for, and committed to, equal opportunities for America's marginalized and dispossessed, including African-Americans.

I began to understand that people like my parents, in faraway places, had been no less fascinated by him than were the American people. Kennedy, it seemed, embodied a special quality of idealism that was appealing to people everywhere.

My parents, without the benefit of television or the Internet, knew about President Kennedy and his children, Caroline and John, and they fretted about them having to grow up without their father. It seemed inevitable that almost as soon as I started grade school, I began to read the books I found at home and in the library about the fabled family. Over time, I too became enchanted by the Kennedy lure—the lure of Camelot.

So, even though John F. Kennedy was long gone and several presidencies removed by the time I got to America, I felt like I was visiting *his* White House. I envisioned myself going to a castle, home to the twentieth century's most alluring and idealistic court; a place where power and beauty converged and reigned, and dreams of a brave new world conceived and burned brightly if even for a fleeting moment.

—॥८—

T he girls pinched me out of my dream. It was just another trip for them and they were certain it would not be worth the walk in the December chill from the nearest parking garage a few blocks away. I held their hands firmly, willed myself to stop the chattering in my head and walked briskly toward the gate.

We joined a fast-moving line, cleared security and were soon inside the building. Barely able to contain my excitement, I followed the line through the hallway, into the oval- shaped Blue Room, the center of the state floor of the White House. Historians say the room, which offers an expansive view of the south lawn, was inspired by George Washington, the nation's first president, and it remains a favorite place for sitting presidents to receive guests. Furnished in the French Empire style,[12] the room was first used following the rebuilding of the White House after its destruction by British forces in 1814, two years into the War of 1812. Sapphire drapery, silk upholstery, chamois-colored wallpaper with imprints of burnished gold medallions, and an oval carpet of predominantly blue, are among the items connecting the room to its name.

Next was the Green Room, said to be the favorite of First Lady Helen Taft, wife of President William Howard Taft. Its serenity belies the fact that this was where President James Madison signed America's first declaration of War—the same war that eventually led to the burning of the White House by British troops in 1814. The room is furnished in the Federal style[13] and contains Daniel Webster's sofa and John and Abigail Adams' silver tea urn. The walls are hung with a moss green watered silk fabric, chosen by First Lady Jacqueline Kennedy in 1962, and the floor is covered with a rare green Turkish carpet.

The Red Room, the next stop, was named by President Rutherford B. Hayes. It is said to be a favorite of most presidents and first ladies because of its small size and bright colors. The walls are covered in red silk twill and the furniture upholstered in red with patterns of gold medallions and fruit baskets. The floor is covered with an early

19th century French Savonnerie rug in shades of red, cream and sage.

Jacqueline Kennedy, wife of President John F. Kennedy, was said to have liked the room so much that she used a painting of it on her Christmas cards in 1962. It is also symbolic of First Lady Eleanor Roosevelt's activism; she used it to host women reporters who were not then allowed to attend White House press conferences.

Even in the face of this amazing history, Ilsa would strike a note that would make the trip especially memorable. Inside a corner, a fully costumed life-size Santa Claus sat detached from the activities in the room. I passed him by, not at all interested in what or who he was. A fellow tourist, however, was more interested and wondered aloud whether he was real or not, meaning was it man or mannequin beneath the red-and-white suit?

Ilsa, who interpreted the question conceptually, immediately spoke up.

"Of course not," she said, her tone wondering what self-respecting adult could even ask such a question. "Santa Claus is not real."

But this one was. In retrospect, he was more than likely a member of the Secret Service, dressed as Santa in the spirit of the holiday, discreetly watching the tourists from behind his festive suit. Intrigued by this show of cynicism in one so young, the man in the Santa suit confronted his tiny detractor.

"So you don't believe Santa Claus is real?" he asked in a dramatic, otherworldly whisper.

"No, you're not real. You're just dressed up," she retorted, neither impressed nor alarmed by a talking Santa Claus in the White House.

The crowd tittered.

"But I bring you presents at Christmastime," countered Santa Claus.

"No," she said, shaking her head definitively. "That's just make-believe. It's the parents buying all the presents!"

The room roared, loud enough for those who were already out of the room to come back in search of the reason for the outburst of mirth.

I smiled, half-amused, half-embarrassed but wholly certain that if any five-year-old was going to challenge the authenticity of Santa Claus, inside the White House, it would be Ilsa. It was entirely within her character, and Alya's too, to take even a tour of the White House and make it theirs.

Outside on the front portico, we exchanged cameras with the only other black family in the group. They took our pictures and we took theirs and went on our way. Other members of the touring party called after my children all the way back to the parking garage, the laughter Ilsa had inspired obviously still on their minds.

July 4, 1999, dawned sunny and glorious. Our second invitation to tour the White House came only that morning and we jumped at the chance to go again on America's Independence Day, and in warm weather. We arrived downtown via metro, joined the line outside the gate and fed peanuts to a frisky family of squirrels while we waited to clear security.

This time, ours was a private tour consisting only of five people—Omarosa, her mother Theresa Manigault, Alya, Ilsa and me. We wandered through the building, watched but unhindered by White House security. The door to the Oval Office was opened but cordoned off with a nylon rope. I hung my body as far as possible inside as I could to see the President's desk, and Betty Currie's office in the back, made infamous by the scandal involving President Clinton and a White House intern, Monica Lewinsky, the year before.

From there, we wandered inside the empty Cabinet Room. Since cameras were not allowed, we had to make the trip special somehow. It was then that I pulled out the President's chair, sat on it, and savored for a few seconds what it meant to be in that space: Air Force One, more political power than any other human being on earth, and with that the opportunity to influence millions of lives for better or for worse.

Next, we went to Vice President Al Gore's office. We were treated to colas from his refrigerator, before making our way to the south lawn to join a throng of Americans, just hanging out, waiting for the fireworks at nightfall.

Chelsea Clinton, the president's daughter, and her friends

were on the balcony. We waved to them thinking that the day could not possibly get better. It did, when President Clinton emerged from the mansion accompanied by his dog, Buddy. They looked great together, both sleek and handsome, and much better than they did on television.

They played for a while, the President throwing a yellow tennis ball and Buddy bringing it back each time. Then, he began to work the line, greeting those who had chosen to spend America's national day at the White House.

We were a small group—a splash of color among mostly pale faces. He moved purposefully, watching us from the corner of his eyes as if willing us to stay put for as long as it would take him to reach us.

Then, he was there.

"President Clinton, they are from Jamaica," my friend introduced us.

"Really?" he said. "What are you doing in Washington?"

I told him about my studies at Howard University, about Jamaica, about the trade winds and the mountains and how they keep the island insulated from the sweltering temperatures of the kind that Washington was experiencing on that day.

"Well, I am sorry it's so hot in Washington," he concluded, as if he felt personally responsible for the more than one-hundred-degree temperature.

The exquisite fireworks display later turned out to be only the grace notes on a glorious day for me, a mother with two young girls who were nearly always at my feet. They did not quite grasp the implications, but I knew that one day they would appreciate the memories and the photos of themselves at the White House, shaking hands with a sitting president.

On that day too, I appreciated more than ever the graciousness of America in throwing its arms out to the world and challenging all those who dare to come, to help make a great experiment work. And, I appreciated that my daughters and I got to do what most Americans never will: We held the President's hand and we sat in his chair.

ELEVEN

Children: Of A Lesser God?

Keep me away from the wisdom that does not cry.
The philosophy which does not laugh
And the greatness which does not bow before children.

—Khalil Gibran

"**O**h, I can't wait to be twenty years old!"

She was only five years old, but the force with which she threw herself on her bed testified to what seemed like palpable frustration with her life.

"Why? What's wrong Baby?" I asked, hurrying over to her.

"I just want to live my own life," she flung back. "You are always bossing me around."

"Really?"

"Yes!" she asserted. "You are always telling me: Ilsa, do this! Ilsa, do that! Ilsa, don't do this! Ilsa, don't do that!" she mimicked unflatteringly.

My brain went immediately into overdrive. My greatest aspiration for my children was for them to be happy and for them to find that happiness within the sanctuary of their home first of all. Within the confines of home, I believed, they should have all their material needs taken care of, they should feel safe, be at peace and completely free to enjoy the magic of childhood. That to me would be the ultimate test of my success as a mother. Happiness, *joi de vivre*, serenity, faith in a greater power and strength of character are the great intangibles that would allow them to navigate the course of life with fewer heartaches and fewer shattered dreams. Childhood and home were where it should begin.

Until then, I thought I was doing a decent job as mother and caregiver and the most constant presence in my children's lives. But Ilsa was telling me otherwise. She was not happy, and surely her unhappiness, as she was expressing it, had to be my fault and by extension my responsibility to fix?

I began to process the dynamics.

—⁂—

I lsa is a strong-willed child and confident already that she can handle the world. I was *her* mother; more fully aware of how vast and complex the world was and how impossible it is to ever truly understand. Worse, I was constantly second-guessing what I had done— removing them from the culture that I knew, understood and could navigate, and from the protective cocoon woven round them by friends and family in a small society, to the vastness of the United States. Gone was the comfort of having aunties, uncles and cousins "just down the road;" of knowing the neighbors by name as well as the shopkeepers, the bus drivers and the postman. With the vastness of this new society, comes not just impersonality, but a far more complex social, cultural and moral milieu, a context where two little black girls of immigrant parents could so easily get lost in the mix, slapped with a stereotypical label and placed in a box labeled "Children of Single Black Mother," "Likely Runaways," Most Likely to Fail," Not Particularly Important" or "Low Priority."

To compensate, I determined that I had to keep them close to my heart, close to my body even, and I had to engender in them a healthy respect for me as their mother and the ultimate authority figure. How else could I keep them from getting lost in it all?

—⁓—

"I am your mother," I said gently to her now. "I don't mean to hurt your feelings, but it is my job to protect you—to teach you what's wrong and what's right. When I see you doing something wrong, I have to let you know."

"No," she said with disconcerting certainty. "That's not why you do it. You do it because you think you know more than I do. You think because you are bigger than me, that your spirit is bigger than my spirit. But if you could come into my body and let me come into your body, you will see that my spirit is just as big as yours!"

She flung the words at me with a force that left me more than a little rattled. She was right on at least one count, I decided: I did think I knew more than she did; I thought so as a matter of course. I was the adult, and she, a mere child. The rest of it, the size of my spirit, versus hers, I had not really thought about. Now, I was forced to think hard about that too—about whether I was confusing the size of her spirit with that of her body and whether by my responses, I was communicating that hers was not quite as good as mine because mine was *bigger*.

Maybe I was. Maybe I had fallen into that same human trap of placing more value on bigger, older bodies than on tiny, young ones. It is a common phenomenon and one of the reasons that thousands of children, throughout the world, become victims of indiscriminate violence and physical, sexual or emotional abuse every year on a daily basis. Many of them will die and many more will become emotionally and physically scarred for the rest of their lives. Some of these children will be forced to work to help support the adults in their lives. All of them are linked by the common bond of their helplessness as tiny bodies.

—⁓—

The United Nations consistently condemns the state of the world's children. *Childhood Under Threat* was the title of its 2004 annual report. *Invisible and Excluded*, it said in 2006. The reports paint a bleak picture of childhood all over the world: millions of children have no adequate shelter, sanitation, access to safe water or health care services. More than one hundred million children have never been to school and nearly as many are starving. In 2003, the United Nations International Children's Emergency Fund reported that worldwide, some thirty-five hundred children under the age of fifteen, die from child abuse. Spain, Greece, Italy, Ireland and Norway have the lowest incidences. Incidences of death from child abuse are six times as high in Belgium, Czech Republic, New Zealand, Hungary and France, and ten to fifteen times as high in the United States, Mexico and Portugal. Overall, thirteen out of every one thousand children in the United States suffered some form of abuse. Of that number, 11.5 per cent suffered sexual abuse, 22.7 percent physical abuse, and 53.5 percent from neglect. An estimated one quarter of victims suffers more than one form of abuse, and more than 1,000 will die as a result.

—⟨⟩—

My children's lives seemed picture perfect by comparison and rightly so, as I had no desire to hurt them, and I tried hard to be a good mother. But clearly, something about my interaction with them, or with Ilsa at least, had been undesirable enough to warrant her backlash.

It would have to be her. Of the two, she was the more cerebral. Her impatience with emotionalism was often disconcerting in one so young. She was the one who, when I repeated a compliment to her from one of her teachers, responded, not with the expected childish delight, but with a laconic: "I have been going to school all my life! Shoot! What do they expect?"

Another time, I tried to impress upon her the importance of giving, and sharing with others.

"You have to learn to share," I told her. "I promise you, you will never experience real joy in life until you learn how to give. I know and I would not lie to you."

Just to make sure she understood, I got down on my knees beside her, put my arms around her shoulders, looked directly in her eyes and sang:

Love is something if you give it away,
Give it away, give it away
Love is something, if you give it away,
It comes right back to you.

It's just like a magic penny,
You put it in your pocket and you don't have any
But if you spend it or give it away
It comes right back to you, Hallelujah!
It comes right back to you.

She was quiet the whole way through and I took it as a sign that she was paying attention. Satisfied that I had made an impression on her, I let her go and waited for a reaction.

"Mommy," she said promptly. "I think you have been watching too much Oprah!"

I slowly began to understand what my friends meant when they told me that Ilsa had been here, in this life, before—an old soul in the body of a little girl. Her confrontation with me now was a request that I acknowledge that.

"I am sorry, Ilsa," I said sincerely. "I won't boss you around anymore. I didn't realize that that was what I was doing."

She stared at me for a moment, her eyes flashing black fire. Then, apparently deciding that I was contrite enough, the rigid lines of her body relaxed and the smallest hint of a smile played at the corners of her mouth.

"Okay," she said.

"Gimme a hug?" I asked cautiously.

She complied before sauntering off to the living room to watch the "Big Comfy Couch" with Loonette the clown and her doll Molly.

In the ensuing years, I would have many other experiences that would turn my preconceptions about the parent-child relationship upside down. That day, however, was a defining moment for me. I began to think more consciously about my children as full-fledged human beings, even if they were young, small and dependent on me for much of their care.

Indeed, it was the beginning of a conscious recognition that they are not mine to own, but to hold in trust; that, to paraphrase Khalil Gibran, though they come from me they did not belong to me; that respect in the parent-child relationship was a two-way street, independent of the status of the one or the other; that their souls were at once great and fragile and that my role as a mother was a sacred responsibility and one that I had to exercise with great care.

TWELVE

Girl In Blue Jeans

May you build a ladder to the stars and climb on every rung

—Bob Dylan

Levi Strauss and Jacob Davis struck gold in 1873, the year they riveted men's pants to strengthen them. They patented the process and jeans were born. Since then, jeans have arguably become fashion's most universal item. Men and women all around the world wear them because they are comfortable, utilitarian and even sexy, some say. My daughter Ilsa wore them for all of those reasons, and for one far more profound as I would soon discover.

She was ten when she told me why she wore blue jeans to school all the time. Right away, I knew it was past time to gently close the door on the briefest of yesterdays when she was a little princess wearing frilly dresses in pink, white, green and yellow.

"I have to play kickball, Mommy," she explained patiently for the umpteenth time as she wriggled into her jeans and dismissed the skirt or dress I held in my hand. "Skirts just don't work for that."

Her answer was the same each time I tried to get her to wear a dress, but I pressed on anyway. After all, they were growing up so fast. There was, around my heart, a growing sense that they had already outgrown wearing cute little spring dresses from K-Mart, signaling the end of childhood.

With her steely grit evident from a very young age, Ilsa won the arguments about what to wear all the time. Usually, I retreated thinking that one day I would present her with the one perfect dress that she would not be able to resist. In the meantime, I had to choose what was worth fighting with her about or what required gentle persuasion on my part. Getting her to choose a dress over her pants was not worth a fight no matter how much I wanted her to look a little more "girly."

Late in the spring of her fifth-grade year, I tried again. Things were getting pretty hopeless now with her having only a few weeks left in elementary school. I chose an insanely beautiful day with the bright yellow sun pouring forth from overhead, the trees a lush mid-spring green and birds singing happily outside to try again to get to put on a dress. It was a Friday too, a perfect day for wearing something different from the weekday jeans and tee shirts.

As far as school days go, Fridays were lazy ones in my mind. Back when I was growing up in Jamaica, Fridays were the days that many people took the children out of school to help on the family farm, sell produce in the marketplace or help with chores around the house. For those of us who actually went to school, things were different too. Devotions were extended to an hour of singing choruses and reciting Bible verses. Further, because there were far fewer children in school than other days, our activities were more fun than serious—like mentals, quick calculations in our heads, instead of mathematics, and spelling instead of English. Sometimes the classes were so scanty, the teachers merged two and sometimes three grades to make sense of holding classes.

On Fridays, we also exchanged our uniforms for casual clothes. Decades later and a world away, I was still partly in that mind-set.

"Come on Ilsa. It's Friday," I said. "Wear a dress for a change."

"But I play kickball *everyday*," she said emphatically, ignoring the dress I was holding out to her.

"Every day?" I asked incredulously.

"Yes, Mommy. *Every day.*"

She was not about to budge, I could tell. Reluctantly, I gave in to wisdom's soft whisper, telling me yet again this was not a battle worth fighting. I did not know then that very soon, I would be rewarded with a lesson in the real reason for her aversion to the garments little West Indian girls traditionally wore, a lesson that would make me far more proud than sorry.

"Mommy," she said that morning as I walked with her to school and seemingly a little sorry that she could not satisfy my desire to see her in a dress. "Do you know why I play kickball?"

Why did we—my siblings and I—play jump rope, hopscotch, cricket or dandy-shandy? There was no deep reason behind it as far as I was concerned. We played because we had no televisions to watch and no video games or computers. We played because our parents had neither cars nor money to take us anywhere. We played because we were not old enough to be entirely responsible for the cooking, washing, cleaning or minding the goats, chickens or pigs. We played because, like most children, we were so wired, unable to sit still for too long. We had to satisfy our insatiable appetite to run and jump, even if it meant skinning our knees or breaking our toes every so often. We played because we were children and for children everywhere in the world, playing is a rite of passage that makes childhood, childhood.

My daughter asked the question, however, in a tone that suggested there was a deeper meaning behind her kickball than there was behind the dandy-shandy of my childhood. I was bursting with curiosity. After all, this was what was getting in my way of having her wear a dress or a skirt every so often and looking like a young lady rather than a tomboy.

"No," I said aloud. "Why don't you tell me?"

"To beat boys, Mommy," she said passionately. "To beat boys."

I looked at her in alarm. I did not know her to have a violent streak. Plus she should not be beating *anyone* and most definitely not at school.

"I don't mean it like that," she said quickly, laughing a little at my reaction. "You know, a lot of the boys in my class have this attitude that just because we are girls, we are silly and we can't do anything right. They think that just because they are boys, they are better at everything. I beat them in class all the time, but I have to show them that I can beat them on the field too. I have to show them that I can run just as fast and

just as hard as them. So, that's why I play kickball, Mommy. And that's
why I have to wear my jeans. It just works better."

All parents have moments like this—moments when their love
and respect for their child or children overflow to the point where their
chests could just explode. For me, this realization that Ilsa was not only
discerning enough to recognize one of the great battle of the ages, but
she was saying quite plainly that she was prepared to fight against any
notions of herself as less than an equal because of her gender. In fact,
she was already fighting—with her intellect and her jeans.

I was squarely on her side and on the side of wearing jeans
forever as long as she was prepared to use them to fight discrimination
against women in particular, and the marginalized and the oppressed
in general.

Here in America, I soon realized, much attention is paid to
discrimination on the basis of race, ethnicity, and increasingly religion,
but far less so to that which is gender-based. Although there is legislation
against all forms of discrimination, gender-based discrimination often
goes overlooked—maybe because it is so much a part of history and
tradition, so insidious, it passes as *normal*. It accounts, for example,
for why women are paid less than men in the workplace and why even
though the facts exist to support that there is obvious discrimination in
this area, there is, in general, not much outrage about it.

Discrimination against women accounts too for why the
United States has not yet had a woman president. In spite of its surface
appearances of intellectual sophistication, the country is yet to evolve
in many ways, particularly at the level of individual attitudes. This was
certainly obvious in discussions around Hillary Clinton, for example,
during her tenure as First Lady, later as a senator and in her failed bid
for the White House.

While few doubted that she was capable of being an effective
leader, discussions in the media around her presidential bid, invariably
seemed to see her gender as a hugely decisive factor—not a particularly
progressive position, considering that we are nearly a decade into the
21st Century. Similarly, when she was First Lady, the subtext of many
discussions seemed to suggest a society uncomfortable with a woman

who was a wife and mother, who also possessed a powerful intellect and the desire to use it.

Although the British bettered the Americans by electing a woman, Margaret Thatcher, as prime minister and allowing her to rule for 11 years from 1979 to 1990, the overall picture is not much better in that country. Sixty-five percent of British companies had no women on their board at all up to 2003 and no British woman has yet headed any of its big companies, although nearly half the workforce is female.[14]

Elsewhere in the world, women's access to resources is extremely limited and their opportunities for higher education and training concentrated within very narrow, service-oriented fields. Polygamy is also widely practiced in some religions, including Islam even though Muslim scholars say the Koran, the Islamic holy book, warns against the practice if its men are not able to treat the women with justice. Some Muslim countries, most notably Tunisia, have banned the practice completely.

In the workplace, the so-called glass ceiling—the artificial cap placed on women's abilities and aspirations to leadership, remains very much in place, albeit with increasing cracks as women butt their heads against it. Although women hold nearly half of America's jobs and more than half of all masters degrees awarded, for example, most senior managers are men. The small percentage of female managers earns, on average, 68 percent of the income of their male counterparts.

Violence against women is yet another way in which gender-based discrimination and male chauvinism manifests itself. The World Health Organization (WHO) says this is a persistent problem all over the world; one in every three women is beaten, coerced into sex, or abused in some form. Further, millions of women are "missing" from the world today as a result of abortions of female fetuses and the murder of female newborns, and male partners are responsible for an appalling 70 percent of female murder victims.[15]

At the policy level, decisions that affect women continue to be made mostly by men, even those about health and contraceptives and gender specific resources they need to have access to.

I was sad that my daughter was growing up in a world where

equality and justice are still elusive for many people because of their race, social class, ethnicity, skin color, gender and other accidents of birth. I was sad too for the little boys in her class, who at their age, have already learned to be cocksure about male "superiority" and by extension, to be condescending to the opposite sex. It was especially disheartening because male chauvinism is learned behavior. This means that someone, somewhere in the lives of those little boys was teaching them, consciously or unconsciously, to disrespect women or at the very least, to disparage their abilities. Such attitude, left unchecked, will result in the continued subjugation of women well into the 21st century.

Underlying my sadness though was immense hope borne of Ilsa's courage and a feeling of triumph that she is among the women of the future who, with the intensity of the fire of righteousness blazing inside, will render sexism, racism and all the other "isms" we have conjured up to make some people's lives miserable completely obsolete. I welcome every pair of jeans as an ally in the fight.

THIRTEEN

To Thine Ownself, Be True

To be nobody but yourself—in a world which is doing its best night and day,
to make you everybody else—means to fight the hardest battle which any
human being can fight; and never stop fighting.

—e.e. Cummings

Alya is growing up and getting some real lessons about life, and she is mad as hell. Her middle school, Colonel E. Brooke Lee in Silver Spring, Maryland, was providing a fertile ground for many of the challenges she would have to contend with in her life as an intelligent black woman in America. When the school decided to sponsor a Black History Month essay competition, she entered and used the opportunity to put her most pressing thoughts on paper. She placed third and got a check for twenty-five dollars, which she decided to keep as a souvenir instead of cashing. I put it inside my photo album, next to the armband the nurse put on her when she was born at 12:30 p.m. on January 30, 1991. Then, I read her essay again thoughtfully, pondering the challenges of being one's self when others are determined that you should be their expectation of whatever label they have placed on you, no more and no less. She wrote:

It's the year 2004 and although bathrooms, water fountains, and restaurants don't boast the large "Whites Only" signs that they once used to, we are not that far from lapsing into another cycle of segregation. We have come a long way, but we still have to fight the temptation to put people into little boxes because of their sex, skin color or ethnicity, or age.

Schools are integrated, people all use the same facilities, and blacks are no longer denied the rights of a free society that were promised to them at the end of the Civil War. Despite all of this progress we have made, there is a long road ahead and we cannot let our guards down. We have still not yet achieved the equality strived for by our predecessors.

On September 11, terrorist attacks left our country confused and scared. We initially came together to help prevent another attack and diminish the fear left behind, but after that our confusion turned to anger and contempt toward Muslims and people of Middle Eastern descent. Innocent children were being targeted and labeled terrorists. In airports, Muslims were subjected to extra long searches and "random" security checks. But, alas these checks weren't random. We were once again targeting instead of embracing differences.

Even at this very moment, a group of people is being disrespected and ill treated because of their sexual orientation. Hearing about another hate crime against a homosexual is nothing new. Although you are entitled to your opinion, why should you take it upon yourself to tell them that they are wrong by saying mean things or hitting them? It is this complete disregard for people who are not the same, which stops us from reaching our social goals.

Even at E. Brooke Lee Middle School, walking the halls, racial slurs can be heard. Black children who try to make the best of their free education by paying attention and striving for good grades are labeled as "white" (It's an insult). If you wear the right clothes and master your slang you're "black" and therefore cool. People who are black but "act white" are called Oreos (as in black on the outside, white on the inside). If you are white but act "black," you are an Uh-oh Oreo. Isn't that clever? If only kids applied this creativity everywhere.

Black people are on top of the gang food chain and are known as the toughest and most hardcore. Then the Hispanics are second. Asians are third (because of the popular stereotype that they can all do karate (see what I mean). See a pattern anyone?

If you've achieved the correct level of "blackness" even if you are white, kids greet each other as "nigger." For example, "What's up nigga?"

is the greeting nowadays. What ever happened to "hello?" Or "good day?"
White kids are taught to resent rather than embrace their culture and black
kids have it embedded that to be accepted as black, you can't be too smart or
the other kids won't like you.

There is something terribly wrong with this and it should not be
tolerated. If teachers hear a kid call another a "bitch" they are usually referred
or some action is taken. But if they hear another student say "Stop acting
so white" they aren't as quick to intervene. They aren't sure if they should
and sometimes the indecision is written clearly on their faces. Well teachers,
you should.

—⧲—

My grandmother died when I was twelve. But somewhere
before that, between age six when I went to live with
her and the time she passed, she taught me what was important in life:
character, hard work, honesty, integrity, self-respect and the dignity
that is completely inherent in my humanity. The color of my skin was
never mentioned—not as a reason for special treatment and not as an
excuse for lack of ambition or failure to dream and build. I have tried
to live her values, refusing throughout my life to be defined by race,
gender, social class or material possessions, regardless of how others
have sought to impose limitations on me, and I have tried to teach my
children the same.

Quite often, the world has entirely different expectations of
who we are, as my daughter was finding out. As a black child in America,
for example, she was expected to conform to a certain mode of being—
much of it senseless, unproductive and coming most often from other
black children, influenced by their own set of experiences and an overall
superstructure within which they must conform to a particular stereotype.

The notion that black children are supposed to be "ghetto,"
for example, is commonly accepted, among blacks and whites alike.
Translated, this means an inability to speak English competently, an
affinity to rap music and BET and MTV, a lack of desire for any kind

of meaningful existence including studying hard, going to college and having a career, and a preference for certain modes of dress that identifies them as black, almost as much as the color of their skin.

Black and poor as they are, my children do not fall into these categories. On the contrary, they are smart and hard working and not ashamed of it; they have always spoken "the Queen's English," and had no access to BET since I did not subscribe to cable television for much of their childhood and teen years. That was a no-brainer; I had no intention of paying another bill to bring something into the house that I would have to turn around and supervise. As for college, the one question that repeatedly came up was "which one?" never whether they would or not.

As time passed, Alya's frustration with her middle school became palpable. I suffered through it with her, bemoaning the fact that I had no choice, especially after I made a desperate run to St. Andrews Catholic Preparatory School one day. The school was located next to her public school and after spending a few hours following her around her classes, I felt like I had to take her out immediately. I checked with the office at St. Andrews and found that tuition for the year was almost as much as my entire annual graduate assistant stipend. She would have to remain in her public school.

At the end of middle school, however, I made the drastic decision to take her out of the public system. I say drastic because I still had no money to pay for it. Although her father had just completed law school and I, a doctorate, our advanced training had yet to translate into meaningful careers for either of us—first generation immigrants struggling to overcome obstacles implicit in our status. I cherished the hope that one day I would have a real job but by then, I knew, it might very well be too late for her. Gambling with credit card debt, rather than her future or her emotional and social well-being, was a better way to go.

In the fall of 2004, she entered Our Lady of Good Counsel, a private preparatory school sponsored by the Xaverian Order of the Roman Catholic Church, in Wheaton, Maryland. She began with a different kind of trepidation: With a population of just over twelve hundred, the school was predominantly white with a sprinkling of Asians, blacks and Hispanics. Although she was happy to be leaving the rough-and-tumble world of public school behind, she was anxious that with so few blacks, she might not make any friends.

Silently, I shared her worries too, concerned that in attempting to place her in an environment more conducive to learning, I may have been exposing her to social isolation. After all, just because we were clear in our minds about how we relate to the world did not mean that the rest of the world felt the same way. Because this was a private school, I worried that she might be isolated not only on the basis of race, but social class. How many other parents, I wondered, could possibly be paying their school fees with credit cards?

"You will be fine," I assured her, determined not to be undone by any misgiving. "Moreover, don't just look for black kids to be your friend. I will bet you that there is a little white girl, a little Spanish girl or a little Asian girl there who is scared and looking for a friend just like you are. You need to find that kid because when you do, you will have a friend."

Faster than I had time to think about it, her new friends were trooping in and out of the house and calling to me in the school parking lot. They came in different shades and hues: Jenny, Mexican; Alex and Ariel, African-American; Julie, African-American with roots in The Cameroons; Katie, tall and blond; Casey, tiny, brunette and Catholic; Tara, another tall blond; Steph, a redhead; another Katie, brown-haired; Zach, blond and adorable; and Jeff, dark-haired and completely wonderful.

Hair color became my best asset in helping me keep abreast of names and faces. Beyond that, I found myself facing one challenge only—restraining her from signing up for every club and every after-school activity available at her school: speech and debate, the peace and justice team, the soccer team, which she eventually managed for two years, among others.

I had little doubt that my daughter had found her niche or that she had fallen in love with Good Counsel. Grounded in the principles of the Xaverian tradition, the school's philosophy is that: each person is uniquely created by God and possesses special abilities and interests that must be recognized and developed; the education of all students should be challenging, technology enhanced, and goal oriented; students with diverse learning needs will be academically successful in an environment where they search for meaning, appreciate uncertainty, and inquire responsibly; the education of the whole person occurs through cooperation and collaboration among students, parents, faculty, staff, and administrators; lifelong learning is fundamental for constructive and responsible participation in a diverse and changing society; and students will learn effectively in an educational community that is safe and nurturing. I concurred, and seeing her bounce out of bed in the mornings, smiling and ready for the challenges of a new day, was all the validation that I needed, despite the financial hardships.

Finally, Alya felt liberated enough to see her capabilities as parallel to her dreams. Finally, the desire to do well did not set her apart, did not mean she was "acting white." Finally, she was in an environment where the majority of children were too focused on their own goals to pay attention to her weight, her clothes or the way she spoke. Finally, getting dressed for school every day of the week meant a khaki skirt, navy blue polo shirt, navy blue socks and black oxfords. There would be no drama about clothes, about hair, make up or brand-name sneakers. Finally, she could just go to school to learn and be herself.

Ultimately, Alya's experience would not be perfect, despite its many positives. Life, by definition, is imperfect. This, however, does not absolve us from the responsibility to attempt to correct imperfections or to make a good life better, especially when those imperfections go against the core tenets of what we say our belief systems are.

Routinely, Alya would describe the school community as being steeped in racist ways—the kind that is so insidious, it mostly goes unnoticed. One day, for example, she came home in deep pain, stung by some of her classmates' reactions to her history teacher's description of Jim Crow and segregation and what African-Americans had to endure.

"They laughed, Mommy," she lamented. "They laughed, and I don't see how anyone could find it funny. Racism is not funny. Cruelty to other human beings is not funny. I mean, I went to the bathroom and cried."

The tears were welling up in her eyes again, an expression of great anguish from a child who did not cry easily. I fully understood it.

No one should laugh about Auschwitz, because it was not funny, nor will it ever be. No one should laugh about Rwanda, because it was not funny, nor will it ever be. No one should laugh at the destruction of the Murrah Building in Oklahoma in 1995. No one should laugh at the attack on the World Trade Center and the Pentagon in 2001, and no one should laugh about slavery and Jim Crow because laughter suggests complicity and only when we recognize these events as among the deepest of human tragedies, can we be assured that similar ones will never happen again anywhere in the world.

My daughter understood what her classmates did not, and it pained her deeply.

"What did the teacher do?" I asked, absorbing some of her distress. I hated to see her hurt and crying like that.

"Nothing," she said. "I don't think he even knew what to do."

"Would you like me to go down there and talk to him a little? I mean, I expect the teachers to have a certain sensitivity."

"No," she said. "I can handle it."

Since then, she has done just fine, embracing her school in all its richness while devising her own practical and emotional strategies to deal with those aspects that are behind the times.

On May 16, 2006, the conclusion of her sophomore year, Alya summoned me to a recognition ceremony at her school. She collected two awards that day; the first for general leadership within the school community, and second for her role as co-founder of the Polish Club. The latter evoked curious response from the audience. Wasn't there something even just a little incongruous about a black child passionate about a culture so far removed from her own?

But it was not incongruous at all. Not for Alya. Not for this black child who has learned to face life, shoulders back and head up and looking the world squarely in its eyes. Not for a child who has learned that the black skin she was born in does not make her any less a part

of humanity. Not for a child who has learned to embrace the world—
to resist the temptation to face it merely as descendants of slaves, but
as a full-fledged human being. And, not for a child who was taught
that before her ancestors were taken out of Africa, before the Middle
Passage, before they arrived in the New World in chains, before they
were slaves, they were human beings.

FOURTEEN

Those Who Have Not Sinned

May you find serenity and tranquility in a world
you may not always understand.

—Sandra Sturtz Hauss

"Abortions are wrong, Mommy, right?"

Amidst the noise in the media, Alya sought my opinion on this important life issue. Although she made her statement with a good deal of certainty, her eyes sought mine, and I recognized in them the need to hear my perspective.

I was elated and humbled at the thought that my opinion still mattered to her. After all, I was just "Mommy," and profoundly aware that as she got older, what I believe, on this and other subjects, will likely diminish in importance, relative to the influence of her peers and her desire to formulate her own opinion. It is the nature of life; our children coming of age coincides with their parents certain march into antiquity. Of course, I knew too that she was eager to see my reaction to the fact that she was siding with the Republican President George W. Bush and disagreeing with Democratic Senator John Kerry. That did not normally happen in our house.

At thirteen, she was charming, well-read, well-spoken and

thoroughly fascinated by the cut and thrust of any debate. She was transparent too and I delighted in watching her refine her positions based on some earnest discussion with her friends or her own research at Wheaton Regional Library, where she spent much of her spare time. On the abortion issue, however, she was absolute, resolute and consistent, long before it became the cause celebre of the 2004 election. All life is sacred, she believed, especially that of the innocent and vulnerable. There was, in her mind, no justification for eliminating it, unless the mother's health was in serious danger.

She was revisiting the issue, influenced by media discussions and the presidential candidates' position on it. Senator John Kerry upheld the "liberal" pro-choice position, that women were the sole owner of the right and responsibility to make decisions regarding their bodies and their lives, including whether or not to terminate a pregnancy for whatever reason. Kerry, a Catholic, argued that life begins at conception but no one had the right to legislate a woman's personal choice and especially not on religious grounds. President George Bush, meanwhile, supported the idea of legislation that would determine when and under what circumstances a woman could have an abortion.

Alya and Ilsa were paying close attention, and I let them. They were growing up and they too would need to find their way among the morass of opinions on both sides of the debate, as well as on other critical issues that would impact their lives as women. Exposing them to the discussions and allowing them to question the prevailing views was an opportunity to examine my own position too, even as I helped them shape their own. Again, I had to revisit the criteria for how I framed my answers: age appropriateness, intellectual honesty, and considerate of the ethical, spiritual and legal implications.

Additionally, the dialogue gave me an opportunity to reinforce my daughter's right to her own opinion and to change it as she gained deeper insight whether through research or through her own deeper life experiences. She needed to understand too the risk of buying into the simplistic dichotomies, such as liberal and conservative, created by the media as a framework for discussions on abortion or other equally complex issues. Such reductionism, I believe, merely ensures that the range of views in between—views that are well thought out and considerate of the multifaceted nature of subjects such as abortion—remains outside of the discussions. This was not good enough for the women I was trying to raise. Besides, I rejoiced that she was comfortable enough to open the discussion with me. That was a world away from the way I grew up.

As a teenager, I had no one, least of all my mother, with whom to discuss the kind of issues that she was raising. My mother was not bad, uncaring, incompetent or even deliberately trying to keep things hidden from me; it was simply the way things were. My culture mostly shunned these kinds of discussions, and my mother did not have the linguistic or social facilities to discuss with her children these highly charged issues related to human sexuality in ways that would be productive and meaningful. She too was product of a culture where things were taboo, just because they were.

My upbringing influenced my decision to do things differently. Rather than clinging to tradition, I committed to being open and honest with my children. The transition was not easy, but armed with a better education and social experiences that my parents never had, I have done well measured against the frequency with which my daughters casually tapped my opinion on everything from condoms to oral sex, virginity, and now, abortions. I framed my responses casually, but I made sure to point out what I thought was important and why.

This question on abortion deserved particular sensitivity, straightforwardness and consideration on my part. I did not want Alya to walk away thinking that having one was something to ever be cavalier about, but I also wanted her to know that if it ever came down to it, she had a right to make that choice.

As I thought about what to say to her, I thought too about abortion and what it entails. Simply put, it is the premature removal of a fetus from a woman's body resulting in its death. When this happens naturally or accidentally, it is termed a miscarriage. This is not the basis of endless discussion on the subject from the pulpit, political platform or Internet sites. Those debates are concerned with the deliberate removal of the fetus performed by a physician for therapeutic or other reasons.

Therapeutic abortions are performed when a pregnancy poses severe risks to the mother's life or her physical or mental health, or where physicians believe that a baby would be non-viable because of severe abnormalities. All other kinds of abortions are considered elective.

Abortion is not a new phenomenon. Research suggests that the practice has been around since as early as the second century. However, modern societies have seen a steady increase with nearly fifty million performed worldwide each year. More than half that number is carried out safely in countries where the practice is legal. Another twenty million take place in mostly developing countries, some of which do not allow the practice.

In places where abortion is legal, physicians have a choice of several methods. Surgical abortions are the most popular choices in the first trimester. A relatively simply procedure, it involves using a manual or electric pump to suction the fetus from the uterus. The dilation and curettage (D&C) method is also standard procedure and involves cleaning the walls of the uterus with a curette, a spoon-shaped surgical instrument with a sharp edge. Chemical or non-surgical abortions are also effective in the first trimester of pregnancy.

Physicians say abortions are safe and simple when performed by a competent medical practitioner before the second trimester. There are some risks involved including possible damage to surrounding organs such as the uterus, bowel or bladder; septic shock, a severe infection resulting in reduced blood and oxygen flow to the body tissues and organs; sterility, or the inability to have future children, and even death. Incomplete abortions can also result in hemorrhage and infection. These risks are generally greater in countries where abortions are illegal and performed in unsafe conditions.

Some research has also linked abortions to developing breast cancer. Doctors say this may be because the level of estrogen increases when a woman becomes pregnant and begins to stimulate breast growth in preparation for breastfeeding. If the pregnancy ends prematurely, the excessive unutilized cells heighten the risk of cancer. Adverse emotional reactions, such as depression and anxiety, are also possible consequences of terminating a pregnancy.

There will never, however, be a consensus on the abortion issue. In fact, it can never be deemed as right, only as legal. This gives the upper hand to those who oppose the practice on religious grounds. Extenuating circumstances like rape or possible threat to the mother's health, should she continue the pregnancy to full term, are not enough to dissuade them. Anti-abortion activists say the legal right to obtain abortions in the United States, codified in the Supreme Court ruling on *Roe v.Wade*, has resulted in the killing of one-and-a-half million babies per year since 1973. Only about one percent of these abortions is as a result of rape or incest.

Religious activists, meanwhile, cite *The Holy Bible*, the sacred word of God to Christians, and the sixth commandment—thou shalt not kill—as the supreme reason why abortions should not be permitted. Still, these same activists will bomb a doctor's office or otherwise maim or kill those who favor women's right to choose. The contradictions inherent in these positions suggest that the vociferous protests of some so-called pro-life activists are about much more than abortions. The need among some men to control women's lives at both individual and general levels are important and often overlooked subtexts in the debate.

Despite the vocal opposition in the United States, however, studies suggest that a majority of people in most countries believe that women should have the right to terminate a pregnancy if they so choose. This includes seventy-one percent in Australia and seventy percent in Canada. In the United States, where the debate has been most fervent, an April 2006 Harris Poll found that forty percent of respondents favored upholding *Roe v. Wade*, and forty-seven percent opposed.

Planned Parenthood, the biggest advocacy group for abortion rights in America, argues that women have had good reasons for choosing to abort for thousands of years. Whenever societies attempt to ban the practice, it merely drives it under ground making it dangerous, expensive and humiliating. Moreover, outlawing abortions is discriminatory and incompatible with the notion of personal responsibility implicit in free societies. Ultimately, the right to terminate a pregnancy for whatever reason is one women should always have, more so in cases of rape and incest and where a full-term pregnancy poses serious risks to the mother's health. According to the organization:

> *At the most basic level, the abortion issue is not really about abortion. It is about the value of women in society. Should women make their own decisions about family, career, and how to live their lives? Or should government do that for them? Do women have the option of deciding when or whether to have children? Or is that a government decision?* [16]

Women, worldwide, choose to have abortions for many reasons. They include not being ready to take on the challenges of motherhood for emotional and financial reasons or unwillingness to deal with the impact of a pregnancy on their career or education. Other factors include instability in their relationships; the social and emotional implications of single motherhood; pressure to have children of a certain gender, usually male; and the lack of access to contraceptives. Of courses, there are those instances where women who have been victims of rape or incest may also wish to terminate a pregnancy.

Some women, perhaps a small minority, may have no compunction about terminating an unwanted pregnancy. These are women who live outside of a moral framework and to whom the act of terminating pregnancies is not much different from disposing of a used condom. They live carelessly and use abortions to dispose of unwanted pregnancies.

The vast majority of women, I believe, live somewhere between those two extremes. Only a miniscule few even have the capacity to be nonchalant about disposing of a fetus conceived inside their bodies, if not through an act of love, through some degree of attraction to another human being. Equally, while many women take a firm pro-life stance, there are many more who understand the challenges of all our lives as women and why some may, at some point, find it necessary to terminate a pregnancy, even if it is the last thing they want to do.

As for the question of when life begins, experts say it has been pondered throughout human history and it is one on which consensus is highly unlikely. Noted biologist Scott F. Gilbert in his essay,

When Does Human Life Begin, argues that the answer has been a changing one throughout history. This is so because perspectives on such a philosophical question are subject to our beliefs, values and social constructs. As societies change, influenced by shifting moral and religious perspectives, or by new knowledge, the answers have changed as well.

Like Alya, I believe that life is sacred but I cannot ever advocate for anyone, except a woman herself, to determine what was the right thing to do with her body or her life at any point in time. I cannot, because I know too well that often the circumstances of our lives are not as cut and dried, nor the personal details as tidy as they are in our dreams. I know too, that in the case of a pregnancy, wanted or unwanted, it is the woman who, in most cases, will be most harshly impacted for the rest of her life. For this reason, it is essential that she must always have the option to make a choice about what is best for her life, and answerable only to her conscience and her God.

Alya disagreed with me.

"No Mommy," she said, "abortions are wrong. In fact it's evil. I believe John Kerry is wrong on abortions. President Bush is right."

I applauded her passion and the strength of her conviction and I prayed her life will unfold in such as way that she can stay completely true to her ideal. More than that, I prayed that in the fullness of time, she would understand and accept that human beings, more often than not, fall short of their ideals—that only rarely does the reality of our lives coincide with our fondest dreams. Such an understanding is integral to having a caring and compassionate attitude toward all people, including any woman, who finds herself at a place where a painful, life-altering decision seems like her only choice.

"I hope you will never find yourself in a position where you have to even consider an abortion," I said. "But if for any reason you ever need one, I hope that the option will be available to you. That is what I believe, and that is all I am saying."

I forbade her from joining the pro-life club at her Catholic school. While I completely respect her views and her passions, I believe that her talents would be best utilized in ways designed to educate and liberate as many women as possible from the injustices and challenges they face everyday—just because they are women.

I didn't think joining the pro-life club would help.

FIFTEEN

Cast The First Stone

If a profound gulf separates my neighbor's belief from mine, there is always the golden bridge of tolerance.

—Anonymous

M ost days I looked forward to going home. Other times, I dreaded it, fearing that I would not have the energy or the patience to cope with the barrage of questions and opinions coming at me at the end of a workday. The need for some alone time—a reprieve from the demands of the day, particularly in those first few minutes of coming home from whatever absurdity had taken place in the office that day or just from the stress of driving home in rush-hour traffic— was sometimes overwhelming. As small as it seemed, it was a wish that often went unfulfilled. There was always dinner to prepare, homework to supervise and two young girls eager to talk about their day.

I signed on for all of that when I chose motherhood—a path that by its nature, will always be a complex mix of pleasure and pain. Once the pain of childbirth is over, for example, there is the infinite joy in the reality of giving birth and caring for a new life, the deep pleasure in seeing the world all over again through the eyes of a young child who happens to be one's own. Just as infinite and as deeply felt are the physical and emotional challenges and the endless worries over their health, safety and general well-being. This is multiplied a million times when circumstances are less than ideal, when money is scarce and when one person is on call all the time to be responsive to the children's needs.

The period leading up to the 2004 presidential election would put all my best instincts to the test. Vibrant and engaged, with more time on their hands than I have had since they were born, Alya and Ilsa were often way ahead of me on some issues. They wanted my opinion anyway.

After all, I represented many things to them. I am their mother and by that fact alone, I represent a different generation—older and on a rapid descent into irrelevance. But, I am reasonably well-educated and, in my coherent moments, I am capable of offering cogent insights into many of the issues in the media or just in our lives. More often than not, I will take a humanist stance, coming down on the side of what I believe will be less painful at a personal level and what course of action will most honor the dignity of the individual and humanity in general. I am heavily influenced too by my belief in a moral framework for one's life founded in Christian theology—in the Ten Commandments:

> *Thou shalt have no other gods before me*
> *Thou shalt not make unto thee any graven image...*
> *Thou shalt not take the name of the Lord thy God in vain...*
> *Remember the Sabbath day to keep it holy*
> *Honor thy father and thy mother*
> *Thou shalt not kill*
> *Thou shalt not commit adultery*
> *Thou shalt not steal*
> *Thou shalt not bear false witness against thy neighbor*
> *Thou shalt not covet thy neighbor's house...or anything that is thy neighbor's*[17]

In the Beatitudes:

Blessed are the poor in spirit: for theirs is the Kingdom of God
Blessed are the merciful: for they shall obtain mercy.
Blessed are the pure in heart: for they shall see God
Blessed are the peacemakers: for they shall be called the children of God.[18]

And in the Golden Rule:

Therefore all things whatsoever ye would that men should do to you
do ye even so to them.[19]

I believe too in the rule of law but not so unwaveringly since history is replete with example of unjust laws that have caused great pain to vast numbers of people. Slavery and Jim Crow in the United States, apartheid in South Africa and sundry nations where laws sanction the oppression of women or citizens who are different from the majority in fundamental ways, are among these examples. In those cases, I pray only for the courage to break them.

But I am a Jamaican too—rural Jamaican born and bred. This covers a multitude of sin: a passion that burns as brightly as the noon-day sun; an inclination toward a tradition that is often far more magico-religious than it is scientific; an epistemology (even with my earned doctorate) often grounded firmly in intuitive knowledge—I know what I know just because I know. I know what I know because sometime ago, way back when, my ancestors said it was so. It was handed down from generation to generation, untested, unchallenged, unproven but wholly accepted as unassailable fact. It is the irrationality of these positions— the contradictions that I am—that my children most want to test sometime. At the very least, they would be in for some good laughs.

Alya, keenly in tune with what I am, knew that the question on homosexuality would be an especially difficult one for me because more than any other issue perhaps, it pits the different parts of myself against each other—the "bleeding heart" liberal against the staid conservative, the traditional West Indian woman of peasant origins against the educated worldly wise philosopher; the homophobic Jamaican against the champion of human rights.

—ɯ—

I grew up partly in a fire-and-brimstone Pentecostal tradition where a big, old God was somewhere behind the clouds, rod of correction in hand, looking down and salivating with glee at the prospect of punishing mankind for its sins. In this tradition, sexual sins are particularly egregious far more so than lying, stealing or even murder, it seemed at times. Still, these strong feelings within the culture of the church about sex was something that one had to arrive at through highly deductive reasoning since talking about the subject directly was taboo—like eating the fruit from the forbidden tree. There were diverse names for the sex act itself and for the body parts generally involved. Mostly, these were said in whispers or in codes. Outside of the church, open discussions about sex and sexuality were no less taboo.

The aversion to talking about sex, however, should not be confused with any parallel reticence about having it. In fact, the culture to a good extent is a promiscuous one. It is not unusual, for example, for one man to have several "baby mothers," or for one woman to have three, four or even five "baby fathers." Plus, very many people, perhaps the majority, seem to become sexually active at a young age. With so much embarrassment surrounding any discussion about heterosexual sex, imagine how much harder it would be to talk about homosexual sex. What could a parent with my particular cultural baggage say to my children about homosexuality?

My framework from early on was to create a different atmosphere for my children, one in which they felt free and unconstrained to ask about anything—no matter how intimate, no matter how strange. While we did not spend an inordinate amount of time talking about sex or sexuality, I know I succeeded up to a point, judging by how often the girls tapped my opinion about some of life's most intimate issues. And, often enough, I have been included in conversations about girls they knew who were "stupid" enough to get pregnant in middle school or high school. I took this as the ultimate indicator that I was doing just fine.

So, should gay people burn in hell?

This was how fourteen-year-old Alya put the question to me one evening during the height of the campaign between John Kerry and George Bush in 2004. She was in the kitchen watching television when I walked in. Her eyes blazed her signature *joi de vivre* as she looked at me, barely alive after a long day at work.

Still, I preened a little, secretly applauding what I regard as my evolution as a human being—my ability to step outside of powerful variables such as culture and religious traditions and try to objectively assess some of their most sacredly held tenets. The fact that I even paused to ponder the question meant that I was already stepping outside of how I was raised. For, had I responded squarely on the basis of any of those variables and any of what I had been taught, my response would have been an immediate, fiery and unequivocal: "Yes. Fire bun! Dem must burn in hell."

Outside of those boundaries though, it was clearly not as simple for several reasons. First, on the basis of common sense alone, my children needed to understand and respect people's rights to live their lives on their own terms, just as they would expect theirs to be respected. Second, they are growing up in a world where the majority of people with whom they share their lives are different in some ways, and many of those differences are factors over which the individual has no control. Third, religions, including Christianity, have their limits, a fact that most practitioners often fail to accept. Indeed, deeply religious people are often the most intolerant. Many of them hold rigidly to the view that their belief system is inherently good, while those of others are deficient in some way. Finally, because the world is not made up exclusively of Jamaicans, Christians, so-called conservatives, or highly educated people, using these measures are not sufficient to provide answers that are either absolute or universal.

Should gay people burn in hell?

My answer is influenced by a composite of factors already described: culture, religion, objective data, and my own gut feeling.

These variables, plus my belief in a moral reference point as a necessary part of how we conduct ourselves as human beings, are fundamental to everything I try to teach my children.

Ultimately, I believe it is impossible to raise men and women of character if we take the view that everything is relative; that there is no black, nor white, only shades of gray, and that it is okay to constantly shift the guardrail on the standards that we set ourselves. As with the abortion question, I regarded this one with equal seriousness as, here too, my answer might shape her attitude toward homosexuals and homosexuality for the rest of her life.

Within my mother culture, homosexuality and homosexuals are deeply reviled generally. The reasons behind Jamaica's well-documented homophobia may never be known as it is inherently difficult to ascertain absolutely what accounts for individual attitudes and behavior. I can surmise, however, that most people are deeply impacted by a world view that is at the intersection of Christian fundamentalism and traditional African beliefs, as well as a culture that revels in machismo. A man who exhibits tendencies counter to the stereotypical characteristics will find himself in a socially and psychologically uncomfortable place. In some instances, he will also be physically unsafe as there is little acceptance of homosexuality as anything else apart from a perversion of the natural laws. Culturally and religiously, therefore, I am pre-programmed to reject homosexuality, which experts say has been in existence for centuries.

—◈—

The first recorded use of the word *homosexual* was in 1869 by Karl Maria Kertbeny, an Austrian-born journalist and human rights activist. But it was Richard Freiherr von Krafft-Ebing, the German psychiatrist and author of the 1886 work, *Psychopathia Sexualis*, who popularized the use of the terms *homosexual* and *heterosexual*. In contemporary society, the term gay is used to refer to male homosexuals; female homosexuals are referred to as lesbians.

Modern society, particularly the United States, is increasingly comfortable with the idea of same-sex relationships. However, research suggests that it is difficult to ascertain the number of homosexuals in the United States or worldwide, as the term is ambiguous, including or excluding bisexuals, for example. Also, many people still will not identify themselves as homosexuals because of the stigma attached. However, the Kinsey Reports (1948), one of the oldest known studies on the subject, says thirty-seven percent of males have had homosexual experiences while four percent of men and up to six percent of women have had exclusively same-sex relationships. More recent studies show much lower figures, however, with four percent of voters in the United States identifying themselves as gay or lesbian in exit polls in the 2004 election.

Theories as to why some people become homosexuals vary. Some scientists attribute it to differences in hormonal imbalances resulting in over-secretion of a male hormone in lesbians, and over-secretion of a female hormone in gays. Simon LeVay[20] and other researchers posit that there are significant differences in the physiology of homosexuals versus that of heterosexuals, and these manifest themselves in critical organs of perception such as the brain, ear and nose. LeVay says, however, that his research did not establish cause and effect between those differences and homosexual orientation, nor did it support the notion that homosexuality is biologically determined. Critics, meanwhile, say LeVay's findings were derived solely from studying the brains of homosexual men who died from AIDS. Other factors, therefore, could have accounted for the perceived differences.

Some psychologists, psychoanalysts in particular, posit that most humans are innately bisexual and most have had homosexual experiences or urges. Rather than the clear-cut categories, therefore, human sexuality is best understood as a continuum with individuals more or less heterosexual or more or less homosexual. Social pressures and traditions, they argue, account for why more people adhere to heterosexuality, the most commonly accepted expression of human sexuality, as opposed to behaving in a manner that more closely resembles their nature, which could either be bisexuality or homosexuality. Other psychologists believe that an individual's sexual orientation is shaped in early childhood and cannot be changed at will. Opponents of all these views say homosexuality is a choice—a repulsive and selfish one indulged to satisfy the basest of human desires without regard for consequences at the level of the individual or in the larger community of humans.

My answer to my daughter, as concisely and honestly as possible, must take in the totality of views around the issue as well as my own desire to see her live a fulfilling life with as little pain as possible—a *normal* life.

—⚭—

"**I** don't support homosexuality, if that's what you are asking," I began. "I am one of those persons who believe that God did not intend for men to be with men or women to be with women, and there are very practical considerations for why I believe heterosexuality is the natural, desirable and acceptable expression of human sexuality.

"The most obvious reason is procreation. Humankind is innately programmed to perpetuate itself and this process cannot be accomplished through individuals of the same sex. The very survival of humanity is contingent on healthy relationships between men and women and a balance between the feminine and the masculine. So, although it is possible that some people may have certain impulses that they cannot control, I still cannot accept homosexuality as a normal alternative to a heterosexual relationship. I believe too that there is a certain level of disingenuousness among people who try to promote it as such. Everything in nature suggests otherwise."

Her thoughtful "uh-huh" encouraged me to carry on, unlike those occasions when she had casually informed me that not every question was an invitation to a lecture.

"The Bible also gives us some guidelines on this. When God thought Adam was lonely, he created a companion for him—Eve—a woman. There are also numerous references in the Bible about homosexuality, none of them condoning it.[21] However, it is important to note that in the eyes of God, there are no degrees of sin. The Bible is no more condemning of homosexuality than it is of fornication, which is sex outside of marriage, adultery or promiscuity. Therefore, to the extent that any society, on the basis of Christian principles, is willing to draw a line in the sand as far as homosexuality is concerned, honesty at every level demands that the same be done against all other so-called moral sins, or sins against the body. Otherwise, objections are grounded in hypocrisy.

"Since I don't hear anybody calling for other "sinners" to "burn in hell," I don't see why that should be the standard for homosexuals. I don't believe they should be set upon, harassed or discriminated against. Rather, I believe like all other human beings, they should be free to live their lives as they choose. Whether or not they should burn in hell is a decision for someone else—the Higher Power, in whose name we condemn homosexuality."

SIXTEEN

Wings Like Eagles

Children are a wonderful gift…. They have an extraordinary capacity to see into the heart of things and to expose sham and humbug for what they are.

—Desmond Tutu

I believe in the value of a good education. Beyond the fact that it offers better career opportunities, and by extension greater financial rewards, it provides the most valuable framework to understanding and interpreting the world and our places in it. This is increasingly important in an age of converging cultures, ethnicities, nationalities and religions. Further, education is the one proven tool in the fight against poverty and its corresponding ills. Far more people will climb out of poverty with a college education, for example, than by winning the lottery, playing professional sports, being an entrepreneur or being an entertainer, combined. Overall, a good education correlates with longer, healthier and more pleasant lives. My desire for a well-rounded education for my children and myself, and all the opportunities that it represents, was the primary reason for my move from my homeland to the United States and for the sacrifices that were a necessary part of that move.

Beyond the formal classroom, I value books as a critical tool in the quest for an education. As such, they were the primary gifts for Christmas, birthdays, grade promotions or any other cause for celebration for Alya and Ilsa. By the same principle, going to the library on the weekend or after school meant an automatic green light as they grew older. Going to the mall did not, unless they were accompanied by a parent or had a perfectly justifiable reason to make a quick trip there and back. Overall, the desire to provide a good education for the girls has been my priority during the past fifteen years, far ahead of buying new clothes, owning a nice car, living in a big house or getting my hair done.

Thankfully, the children fully embrace my philosophy on education and how we live our lives in pursuit of it. Not only do they place a high priority on their accomplishments, but they look forward to celebrating them with me. These could be anything from earning a perfect score on a test to receiving The President's Education Award for Outstanding Academic Excellence at the end of elementary school, as was the case with Ilsa, my younger daughter. Three years later, as an eighth grader in the Montgomery County program for gifted and talented children, Ilsa brought home news that she had been invited to apply for membership in the W.E.B. DuBois Honor Society. Happily, she waited for the official seal of approval from Mommy.

For once, I was not sure and I realized that I had no words for when I was not sure or for when I did not want to burst my girls' bubbles, if I did not have to. I hid my misgivings from Ilsa and told her instead how proud I was—and I was. It seemed like a good thing on the surface, and she was certainly worthy of being selected to any honor society. I was concerned, nonetheless. What was the W.E.B. DuBois Honor Society? Who was behind it? What were the criteria for membership? How many children from her class were invited? Was this an organization for black kids only, or would every child in the school be eligible to join? In short, how would a W.E.B. DuBois Honor Society be conceptualized in the 21st Century?

The answers were very important to me.

William Edward Burghardt DuBois (W.E.B. DuBois) was the first African-American to earn a doctorate from Harvard University and one of the most celebrated black intellectuals and activists of the 20th

century. Academic honor societies, meanwhile, are designed principally
to reward excellence as well as to provide a meeting place for students
with high academic prospects. But I was concerned about how the
founders or organizers had conceptualized a Dubois Honor society, five
years into the 21st Century. Would it be inclusive or exclusive? Would
all the members be selected using the same standards and, if so, what
are those standards?

After ten years in America and being involved in the
education system at different levels, I understand that there are two
sets of standards—one for the mainstream and one for minorities.
The quality of a typical public high school in the District of Columbia,
where the majority of the citizens are poor minorities, for example, is
not comparable to that of their counterparts in the average Virginia
or Maryland suburbs. Since desegregation, many of the schools in the
nation's capital have been run down, understaffed and underperforming.
The children's test scores generally reflect these realities with many of
them performing dismally on standardized tests or other performance
indicators. High drop-out rates is also typical of District of Columbia
public schools and others in so-called urban communities.

At the tertiary level, America's top tier institutions—Harvard,
Yale, Princeton, Cornell, Stanford, Brown, Georgetown, Duke,
and others, are not to be compared or confused with the top tiered
Historically Black Colleges and Universities (HBCUs)—Howard,
Hampton, Morehouse, Spelman, Bennett, and Fisk, among others.
Institutions in the former category, mostly Ivy League, serve the needs
of the elite, including the descendants of former slave owners, while
the latter is the domain of freed slaves and their descendants. The
hierarchy implicit in this arrangement is the very same as that which
existed during slavery and Jim Crow: one group, either on the basis
of race or social class, at the top and another by virtue of those same
variables, but considered to be inferior, is at the bottom.

It goes without saying that the mainstream standards are
legitimate and respected. Minority standards, meanwhile, are widely
perceived as mediocre but they are tacitly accepted in part as concessions
for a history of racism and social inequalities. More importantly, many

minority serving institutions represent a well-needed security deposit against social disequilibrium without necessarily offering real equality in educational opportunities and ultimately career opportunities. The more I understood the system, the more I loathed the hypocrisy it represents and the more I understood how—more than two centuries after the United States Declaration of Independence—the descendants of slaves are still largely marginalized and powerless.

I had no interest in playing along with the status quo or in having my daughters being a part of anything that smacked of concessions or as the inferior version of an accepted double standard. On the contrary, my strategy has always been for them to compete on equal terms and to be at the top, or as close to it as possible. I knew that their innate ability could not be questioned; they simply had to work hard and to be provided the opportunity to reach their potentials.

So, I did not care to have Ilsa become a member of any organization with qualifying labels based on race, social class or ethnicity, particularly when those labels would identify her as deserving, just because she was part of an "inferior" subgroup. Such double standards, I believe, do more harm than good even where their existence is agreed on and accepted by everyone, including those who are being hurt and stigmatized in some ways. While some amount of duplicity may seem necessary given certain historical facts, it is indisputable that the two-tiered education system, especially, also serves to box people of African descent into a very small space. This diminishes their humanity and their rights to all the benefits of community. By the same token, I began to see those who willingly participate and perpetuate some of these traditions as complicit in their own marginalization.

This paradigm would not be a suitable path for either Alya or Ilsa. Rather than contracting their world, I believe I had a sacred responsibility to expand it; to point them to the limitless horizons available to them as members of the human race, fortunate enough to be living in the greatest country on earth. Life lesson number one, as soon as they could understand, was that they were citizens of the world, fully entitled to the respect of all humanity and to all the benefits of the universe. Therefore, they should never allow themselves to be marginalized or treated as inferior because of race or any other variable over which they had no control.

Alya and Ilsa embrace my efforts entirely. I see it in their self-confidence and in the ease with which they embrace people, regardless of their differences. I see it in their endless fascination with languages and cultures other than their own—French, Spanish, Hebrew, Chinese and Arabic. I see it in their burning desire to see the world—from the rolling hills of Ireland to the ancient ruins of Peru; from the great brooding continent of Africa, the land of our ancestors, to the sun-drenched islands of the Caribbean. Europe, Asia, Australia, the Americas, the east, all hold the same fascination for them.

—⁓—

"What is the W.E.B. Dubois Honor Society about? What will you do?" I asked Ilsa.

"I am not really sure, but I know we will go on field trips to different colleges and stuff like that. And, we will help our teachers at school. We will be role models for the other children," she concluded proudly.

Biting hard on my lip, I signed the pile of papers that would get her started on her way. On Tuesday, December 20, 2005, I left work early and went to her school to watch her and fifteen of her classmates inducted into the new honor society.

As usual, I felt great joy just walking through the gates of Eastern Middle School in Silver Spring. On this occasion, like all the other times I had been there, I alternated between wanting to be a twelve-year-old again and wanting to cry for the sheer love of life reflected in the eyes of the children in the humanities magnet. This beautiful program invites students to stretch their imagination, to allow themselves to be all that they can be and to respect the dignity of all people. And, in the bouncing steps and shining eyes of these children, I saw the hope for a better world. Or, perhaps it was merely a reflection of my own dreams that this, in fact, was the greatest generation: the one that will lead the world into a brighter more harmonious tomorrow—free of the baggage of wars, racism, and sexism; entirely life-affirming; and completely liberating of the human spirit.

I settled down to listen.

The first speaker, a seasoned educator, began her address with a tale about a farmer who inadvertently raised an eagle among his flock of chickens without recognizing the odd bird in the midst. A naturalist happened by one day, quickly spotted the eagle and tried to convince both farmer and bird that it did not belong there—had no right to be there scratching the earth like a common fowl. It took some work, but on the third day, the naturalist took the bird to a mountaintop, held it aloft so it could see the vastness of the universe below, and commanded it to soar like the superior creature it was. The great bird fairly grinned at the world unfolding before him. Then with a confident flap of wings, soared into the heavens. The purpose of the W.E.B. Honor Society, the speaker said, was the same as that of the naturalist—to separate the eagles from the chickens.

From where I sat squirming in my chair, it was a bad story, too simplistic even for middle schoolers, particularly very bright middle schoolers, and certainly not what I expected from a highly placed administrator at one of the nation's top HBCUs. I expected her to appreciate the dangers of stereotyping and the inadequacy of her classificatory scheme, and I expected her to have a sense of place and context. In her mind, it seemed, eagles and chickens were at opposite ends of the fowl kingdom. But what about the range of birds in between—the canaries, cardinals, nightingales, larks, sparrows, the tiny versatile hummingbird, and even the scavenging crows?

The range of abilities is even more diverse among children. Some are artists whose brilliance will not surface if they are never exposed to paint and canvas. Some are musicians who will never know if they have never been handed an instrument. Others are scientists, teachers, doctors, engineers, lawyers, chefs, entrepreneurs, and dancers whose special skill may never come to the fore unless a perceptive and imaginative teacher notices their particular genius. Although Ilsa, supposedly, was among the eagles, as an educator and a parent, I was bothered by the unfinished part of the story—the chicken's fate after the lone eagle is taken from the flock.

Common sense tells me that children have differing abilities and interests, which can make teaching difficult even in the best circumstances. This becomes even more complicated in a heterogeneous population with significant differences in languages, socio-economic and cultural backgrounds. In this environment, it is tempting to try to isolate the "eagles" from the "chickens." The "eagles" at least have something in common across the different variables: they are naturally able, self-motivated, quick studies and in most cases, better behaved.

The problem, of course, is that "eagles" are relatively rare, but the "chickens" are abundant. Moreover, evidence shows that African-American children are more likely to be numbered among the "chickens" than they are among the "eagles." The evidence shows too that very often, the performance and placements of African-Americans in the system has little to do with natural ability. It is more often about a lack of resources, less than desirable social environments, a range of attitudes influenced by theirs and their parents' experience of marginalization and racism, and the residual effect of slavery and segregation. For example, it is true that children whose parents have a college education will most likely go to college themselves. African-Americans, however, are still trying to catch up in this area since generations of them did not have the opportunity to go to college. The result, overall, is the so-called achievement gap—the difference in the performance between whites and Asians and African-American children—which educators across the country have been unable to close.

Even middle-class black children in American high schools consistently fall behind their white and Asian counterparts, as countless studies have shown. Examining the gap in 2004, *Time* magazine cited the city of Ann Arbor, Michigan, where the school system spends just over $9,000 annually per student, most of them middle class, with at least one college-educated parent. Despite the similarity in their social circumstances, white children averaged a "B" while blacks averaged a "C." Blacks were also four times more likely to fail a class.

On the Scholastic Aptitude Test (SAT), used as a prime indicator of student achievement, African-American students, in 2004, scored an average 98 points lower than whites on the verbal section and more than 100 points lower in math.[22] According to the College Board,[23] fewer than 2,000 African-Americans scored higher than 1,300 out of 1600 compared to 150,000 others who scored the same or higher. Black males, in particular, are at the highest risk of failing high school, not continuing on to college and failing to graduate even if they do begin.

The trend continues in higher education. Only a limited number of African-Americans are admitted to the nation's top colleges. A study at Harvard University, for example, found that of the 530 black students at that institution, only about one-third of them were African-Americans, the majority being Africans or West Indians. Another study of minority achievement at twenty-eight top-tier institutions, carried out by researchers at Princeton University and the University of Pennsylvania, found that forty-one percent of black students were either of immigrant or mixed race background.

The story about the chickens and the eagles, told by a seasoned black educator at the induction ceremony for the W.E.B. Honor Society, seemed to offer a casual justification of the reasons why so many minority children are labeled as under-performing: they are chickens, not eagles. Taken seriously, the educator's words seem to nullify any reason to attempt to change what is a sad and troubling reality of the education landscape. Based on the paradigm of the educator, the chickens in the system are no more than placeholders, deservedly neglected in favor of the eagles—in keeping with the natural order.

This was a less than auspicious start to the new honor society. The educator, who was also one of the sponsors, did not quite get it. This did not augur well for the new organization.

The function ended. Ilsa walked over and enveloped me in a languid one-arm embrace.

"But Mommy," she said right away. "I just don't get it. I really want to ask, what happened to the chickens after the eagle flew away?"

I breathed a sigh of relief. At least *she* got it. Once again, I was reminded that my hope for the future is in her generation.

"Ask your teacher," I said promptly. "I mean the teacher in charge of your honor society. Ask him, as soon as you catch him in a quiet place."

SEVENTEEN

I'll Fly Away

May the good Lord be with you
Down every road you roam
And may sunshine and happiness
surround you when you're far from home

—Rod Stewart

"Will I still be on your insurance when I go to college?"

Alya, my older daughter, sat wedged between my legs as I groomed her hair. She was fifteen now but she still struggled with doing her own hair. It was thick and strong and wholly unmanageable, as only black hair can be. Since I was never good at grooming my hair myself, even though it was not nearly as thick, I empathized and tried to help.

The question popped up between two strokes of the comb, reminding me that college was only two years away. Since we had started receiving numerous recruiting letters every day, we have been talking about college more often. So, although the question was sudden, it was not out of context.

The thought of her going away to college both excited and terrified me. It was exciting because it meant that, despite the endless challenges, we had both done well in our roles as parent and child, mother and daughter: I worked hard to provide for her, keep her safe, inspire her toward a path that would be meaningful, uplifting and fulfilling, and nudged her little by little toward thinking and acting independently. She played by the rules, concentrating on school and completely ignoring the pull of that other world to which so many young people fall prey. As a result, she was defying the odds stacked against a poor black child, raised by a single mother and preparing for college anyway.

Still, I was frightened at the thought that too soon, she would be gone—facing the world on her own in many ways. More than that, I was beginning to get an empty feeling in the bottom of my stomach, as her childhood was ending much too quickly. I feared that as hard as I tried, I never held her hand long or often enough.

I never read as many stories to her as I wanted to.

We never went to the beach often enough or made enough sandcastles or little balls and dolls out of Play-Doh.

I never played in the park with her enough.

I never once got into that giant slide with her at Wheaton Regional Park instead of waiting at the end to pick her up.

I never plucked up the courage to let her transfer a caterpillar from her hand to mine. Already, it was too late for these things.

So combing her hair at age fifteen was my mommy swan song. It allowed me to hold on to a piece of the little girl I had held in my arms, not so long ago—the little girl who I know is still inside of her, hidden behind a grown-up body and teenage swagger. Back when she was a toddler, and less than two years older than her sister, it seemed that they would never grow up. I thought that it would be eons before I had a full night's sleep, a free moment for myself or even a little part of life that was just my own. Now, those many years have passed, faster than I could blink my eyes, and here she was on the cusp of womanhood, looking forward to departing home to begin *her* life.

I struggled with what felt like schizophrenia.

—ᴍ—

Alya is a free spirit. She wants to go far away, beyond the oceans and the mountains—to London, Paris, Brussels, Sydney, Dublin, Rome, Montenegro, Mumbai, Durban, Johannesburg, Lima, Phoenix, New York, Los Angeles. The whole world beckoned. The whole United States beckoned. Each day, she tried out a different city, a different state, a different country—the more exotic sounding the better. It was clear, she liked the sound of the faraway places tripping from her lips as much as she relished the thought that she would take flight one day and experience in reality what she clearly lived in her dreams.

I am ecstatic at her calm assumption, indeed, her acceptance, that the world is hers for the taking. But I have my own ideas about college: the University of Miami, right next door to my sisters, Lor and Sadie; the University of Maryland, fifteen minutes away from home, or a choice of any of the wonderful schools in the District of Columbia, including Catholic University, fifteen minutes down the road on the red train. Howard University, where I work, would be good too. I would get to see her every day. What excuse could she possibly have for not popping into my office for a chat during her lunchtime?

But she was a wanderer from the day she was born. I could see it in her great big winsome smile, in the way her little eyes sparkled fire at the sight of something new, in her delight in the world and the people around her. Now, the world's pull on her is relentless. She can barely contain her desire to explore, experience diverse cultures, speak their languages and learn their ways. Momentarily, she is tethered to home only by youth, lack of money and the structured world of high school. Those variables will change soon. College loomed and with it more independence than she had ever known.

She was excited but there was trepidation too, as her questions revealed.

"Will I still be on your insurance when I go to college?"

"Uh-huh," I answered.

"Does that mean that you will have access to my medical

records?" she asked.

"Ye-e-es," I answered slowly.

I did not know whether that was true or not but I knew her well enough. I knew that something big was going on inside her head—that the questions were a precursor. I would have to give her answers that would lead her to where she wanted, needed to go. The veracity of my statements could be checked in good time and new answers supplied if necessary.

"But that's not right," she said. "Suppose there's something in there that I don't want you to know?"

"Like what? What could you possibly have in your medical records that you would not want me to know? " I asked innocently.

"Uhhhh. Suppose I have some disease...some sickness that I don't want you to know about?"

"I would hope that if you were ever ill in any way that you would let me know about it. After all, I am your mother," I said quickly.

"Okay, but suppose I get pregnant?"

Now we were getting somewhere, and now I had to pause and think about what she was really asking and what my answers needed to be. My little girl was asking a very grown-up question, initiating a discussion that many mothers, myself included, may be reticent to address.

I am nervous at the very thought of my daughter engaging in sexual activities in the near future—not when she was not quite done reading her Baby-Sitters Club books. Yet, I applauded her candor and her maturity and welcomed wholeheartedly this new opportunity to talk with her about an important life issue.

My mind went back to the way things were when I was growing up. Then, teenage pregnancy was the scourge of many young girls' lives, the great stealer of dreams of lives outside of rural poverty. I recall my first exposure to this social phenomenon, so common in the Third World and among girls in underprivileged circumstances here in the United States.

—〜〜—

L ola, a round-faced gap-toothed girl with olive skin, lived with her grandmother across the street from my family. The grandmother, a cantankerous old woman, swore continuously at the world. As impossible as it seemed, the cursing and the swearing intensified at one point, coinciding with the neighbors constantly whispering Lola's name. Alongside, was the steady growth of Lola's stomach. Based on what I had seen of my own mother and other village women, I discerned that Lola was going to have a baby, but I did not know what she had done to make such a miracle happen.

At fifteen, Lola gave birth to her first son. She had a child nearly every year after that for the next ten years or so.

Then there was Jessie. I was twelve and in the seventh grade at the new government school. She was thirteen and, according to all the teachers, the smartest girl in the eighth grade. There was just one problem: she had a boyfriend who was too old to be in school and too old for her. Soon, rumors began to swirl and the teachers' worst fears were realized— Jessie was expecting a baby. The principal, a staid expatriate from England, was so crushed by her pregnancy and its implications for her future that he did something never done before. He allowed her to remain in school, even as her pregnancy advanced beyond the seams of her blue tunic.

This was not a good idea, as it turned out. I arrived at school one day to see a crowd near the big double doors leading into the main building. Jessie, now around seven months pregnant and wearing a pale blue empire-style dress, had fallen into a half-open manhole near the main door. She was pulled out suffering only from a bad fright and minor scrapes. The birth of her baby boy two months later heralded the end of her education and the death of hope for a life outside of poverty.

There were legions of other girls like Lola and Jessie.

—〜〜—

Alya's questions brought back haunting memories of those days—of my own struggle to avoid the pitfalls of the teenage years in a poor rural community, and get through them with my dreams intact. Now she was at that same vulnerable stage, at risks not just of unwed pregnancy, but of contracting sexually transmitted diseases.

I thought hard about what every young woman needed to know about early, unwed pregnancies—what I needed to tell my little girl to reduce the possibility of her falling into that trap.

The most important fact she needed to know was that pregnancy is nothing contagious nor does it just happen. No one has ever contracted it from a toilet seat or from coming into contact with other pregnant women, and so far, I have heard of only one immaculate birth. Rather, pregnancy is, more often than not, the result of a deliberate action, and a conscious decision to engage in sexual intercourse, typically without using any form of contraception. These include abstinence, the safest and most reliable method, a range of contraceptive pills and injections and condoms, among others. Getting pregnant therefore is highly preventable.

Second, the path of early and unwed motherhood is fraught with complications and stressors that young women should strive hard to avoid. For many, pregnancy often means a premature end to their dreams of a good education because it is extremely difficult to go to college and take care of a baby without money and without a strong support system. The inability to attend college likely will mean that both mother and child, or children, are condemned to lives of poverty.

Third, having an unplanned baby increases one's level of financial, physical and emotional stresses. In addition to worrying about her own future, the young mother must also be responsible for fulfilling a baby's needs. Prenatal and postnatal health care for both mother and child is expensive and can be complicated if the child becomes ill, or is born with a disability.

Fourth, the route to an early unplanned pregnancy is the same to contracting STDs. College students are especially at risk with two-thirds of all new cases in the United States occurring in the

18–25 age group. Genital warts (human papilloma virus), chlamydia, and genital herpes are among the most common. Others include syphilis, gonorrhea, hepatitis and the deadly HIV/AIDS. Chlamydia, a condition that causes unpleasant discharge, vaginal irritation and painful urination in young women, is the most common STD in the United States and on college campuses.

Gonorrhea, chlamydia, and syphilis are caused by bacteria and are relatively easy to cure if detected early. Genital warts, herpes, hepatitis, and HIV are all viral infections and incurable. If detected early, however, their symptoms are controllable with medication. Unfortunately, many college students delay seeking treatment out of embarrassment or because they believe the infection will go away on its own. This can result in complications including pelvic inflammatory disease (PID), infertility, cancer, neurological disorders or worse.[24]

Pregnancies and STDs aside, Alya would need to make good decisions about other high-risk behaviors common among college students. Binge drinking, for example, has been identified as the number one social problem facing students. Reports say close to fifty percent of college students are binge drinkers and only nineteen percent abstain from alcohol.[25] Other dangerous substances such as marijuana, LSD and the designer drug Ecstasy, are all commonly abused on college campuses nationwide. With so much at stake for my daughter, my West Indian ways got the better of me as I began to frame my answer.

"I am not sending you to college to get pregnant," I said firmly. "I am sending you to go get a good education so that you can prepare yourself for life. Getting pregnant in college would seriously complicate your life and compromise your goals. That is up to you, and you have to make sure that that does not happen."

"But stuff happens Mommy."

"Stuff happens because we allow it to. We actually can control stuff. We can do what we have to do to make sure that the stuff that happens is what we really want to happen."

"Okay," she said cautiously.

"Yes, Baby, controlling our impulses is an important part of effective life management," I said. "It's a hard thing, especially when you are a young girl, but you are going to have to be responsible and make the right decisions at the right time. At the end of the day, that is going to be the most important protection you have against all the issues that you will come up against when you leave home."

I swallowed hard. She would be leaving soon whether I liked it or not. She had to because her life was in the big wide world, not in the cocoon of my home, my office, or my car. This fun-loving free spirit who is my daughter would be ill-served without the opportunity to spread her wings and attain the sense of self and fulfillment that all human beings yearn for. College was that wonderful place to begin. She just had to learn to navigate the pitfalls.

"My hope for you is that you will wait for a long time before you engage in sexual activities. Sexual relationships can be very stressful when you are not emotionally ready and when you have other big things to worry about—like getting through college. I hope also that when you decide to, you will be very careful—and you will let me know. Okay?"

"Yes Mommy," she said quietly.

"But, always remember, that if at any time things don't work out the way you want —if you find yourself in any kind of jam, come home to Mommy," I said, the lump growing bigger in my throat. "You know me; I will be upset, and I will let you know, but that won't last. My love for you will always surpass my disappointment or anger at anything you might do."

Her response was heartfelt.

"I love you Mommy,"

"I love you more."

EIGHTEEN

Beyond Words

Do not believe in anything simply because you have heard it...
But after observation and analysis, when you find that anything
agrees with reason and is conducive to the good and benefit of one
and all, then accept it and live up to it.

—Buddha

I missed the first sunrise of 2000. We stayed up late the night before to watch the crystal ball drop in Times Square, performed the ritual champagne toast, noted that at the stroke of midnight the universe was intact and went off to bed. So far, so good.

But maybe Armageddon would begin after midnight. Maybe the break of day would see the unleashing of unsurpassed terror on the land. Or maybe there would be no daybreak. Maybe the first of January 2000 would herald the beginning of one very long, very bleak eternity. Based on the hype in the media, at the very least, a few planes should fall out of the sky; water supply and electricity should be disrupted and personal computers along with computerized services should malfunction.

Close to 10 a.m., on New Year's Day, I awoke to a world drenched in the most glorious sunshine and the earth solidly under foot in South Florida. I switched on the TV to see if the rest of the world was in place and doing as well: Washington, D.C. was still there. Check. L.A. Check.

New York. Check. Lagos. Check. Johannesburg. Check. London. Check. Stockholm. Check. Rome. Check. Geneva. Check. Paris. Check. Buenos Aires. Check. Quito. Check. Cairo. Check. Addis Ababa, Tripoli, Baghdad, Tehran. Riyadh, Tel Aviv, Moscow. Check.

Fidel checked in okay in Havana. Kingston, Jamaica was in situ, eighteen degrees north latitude, twenty-two degrees longitude, and five-hundred-and-fifty miles south of the Florida Peninsula—same place as the day before.

Brokaw, Jennings, Rather, Walters, Chung and Couric checked in to report that there was nothing to report. And now the media had no use for the cutesy little acronym they had coined to make reporting the catastrophe easier: Y2K!

So much for the big meltdown.

In the end, there was nothing—not even a glitch on Amtrak to justify the hysteria in the media leading up to the end of the 1990s and the beginning of the 2000s. Listening to the news and magazine programs though, one would have thought that catastrophe was certain in some parts of the world at least. It was difficult, if not impossible, to look ahead without even a tinge of anxiety given the media coverage.

Mass media affect people that way: They don't necessarily tell us what to think, but by setting the agenda for public discussion, they certainly tell us what to think about.[26]

The media focus on impending catastrophe, in 1999, was hard to ignore. The dire predictions only got worse as the year end drew closer. As hard as I tried, I could not shut it out or shake the thought that something might just go wrong. I stocked my apartment with canned food and drinking water and took off to Florida. There, at least, I would be with family instead of being in Maryland alone with Alya and Ilsa.

—✺—

B efore the Internet, the birth of the printing press in the sixteenth century provided one of the best indications of how mass media could and would influence and change the way people live. Prolific social scientist Ithiel de Sola Pool cited a number of far-reaching consequences of Gutenberg's press. Among them: the rise of the ideas of history and progress, the organization of society around institutions of learning; the rise of libertarian urges; the development of the concept of intellectual property; the development of national cultures; the growth of both science and mysticism; the emergence of modern languages; the separation of the secular and sacred; the codification of laws; an increase in literacy, and the growth of new professions.

The end of the twentieth century coincided with the rapid new development and widespread use of new communication technology all around the world—cellular telephones, satellite television, and the Internet, especially, are uniquely able to eclipse vast geographical spaces and have forced nations to rethink existing laws and traditions. Conceivably, the communications industry, propelled by these new inventions, is the single most important factor driving the phenomenon called globalization—the growing interdependence of the world's people through "shrinking space, shrinking time and disappearing borders."[27]

I know about media—a lot more than Alya does. This is why I have kept a wary eye on the blog she started in her freshman year of high school, long before she even knew that I knew that she had one.

She is as untidy online as she is in actuality. As I have done, since she was a toddler, I walk behind her some, picking up after her, looking out and making sure that she would not harm herself through her own untidiness.

I followed her around online—to the extent that her untidiness allowed me to and that I thought I needed to. For example, she would minimize several windows on the computer screen instead of closing them, forget about them, and go off on her merry way. If I used the computer after her, maximizing the windows allowed me to see where she was or where she had been. Using the browser's back button also allowed me to see the sites she was frequenting.

No, I did not regard it as an invasion of her privacy. Rather, it was my way of protecting her and no different from my picking up objects out of her way when she was a toddler, holding her hands as we crossed the street when she was three or four, keeping her away from the stove, or making sure she did not go into the deep end of the pool before she knew how to swim.

At thirteen, Alya still had much to learn about the world. It would be especially irresponsible of me to let her roam free in the limitless wasteland that is the Internet, considering what I know about the medium; that, for example, it is an infinite warehouse of pornography and other material unsuitable for children; it is a magnet for child predators and worse, its reach is vast—nearly every corner of the world.

—m—

The National Center for Missing and Exploited Children and the Justice Department said, in 2000, that one in five Internet users between ages ten and seventeen had been solicited by a sexual predator in the year before the study.[28] The predators were generally single heterosexual males between the ages of thirteen and sixty-five. They were polymorphous offenders, who preyed on anything or anyone. Experts divide Internet predators into four categories: collectors, travelers, chatters and manufacturers.[29]

The collector seems like the average person next door. Typically, he is a husband and father who stays up after his wife has gone to bed. Seduced by the convenience and anonymity of the Internet, he begins to behave in ways he would not have under other circumstances. His predatory behavior may begin with collecting still photographs of children before progressing to webcams or other interactive media. His last step is making actual contact with children.

The traveler moves quickly from chatting online with children to arranging actual meetings for the purpose of having sexual intercourse. Typically, he is between seventeen and twenty-nine and is willing to travel long distances, even internationally, to meet his prey. His persistence and mobility make him extremely dangerous to young children. He is very likely to send money or provide resources to encourage them to run away from home.

Like the collector, the chatter is a low-grade offender. He gets his thrills purely from talking to children online about sex, but is unlikely to try to make actual contact. This group accounts for the smallest number of predators.

Beyond his interest in sex with children, the manufacturer—unlike other predators—desires to profit from exploiting them. He typically ranges in age from twenty-six to fifty-three and likely has a history of inappropriate contact with children. A child who falls prey to him will likely end up as subjects in pornographic videos sold to other pedophiles. The manufacturer is likely to have the latest model computers and cameras and frequents public places where children are likely to gather.

—⁓—

Despite my well-founded leeriness of the Internet, I did not check up on Alya every day, every week or even every month. She had deposited enough trust and goodwill in her account to render such constant scrutiny unwarranted. But I checked occasionally to make sure that I knew what she was doing. I checked because she was still a young child and like all children was likely to make mistakes. As a parent, my responsibility is to attempt to help her avoid or minimize the most harmful of those mistakes and guide her safely into adulthood. Hopefully then, a greater understanding of life would better inform her choices.

Her blog was innocuous at first.

"School sucks!"

"School really, really, really sucks!"

"There is this really cute boy in my class. I want to talk to him, but I just don't know what to say."

"My Mom finally got a new car—a Camry—so much better than

that piece of crap we used to drive. Now, if she would only learn to drive on the highways!"

"I really, really need some new jeans, but Mommy is being stupid about it."

Alya's blog was so mundane, so typical of a generally well-behaved young girl, that for a whole year, I did not look at it again. Then, I did one day, idly, while I waited at my desk for the clock to strike 5:30.

The mundane stuff was still there, but there were some real changes too. There was much more information about herself and the quality of the language had deteriorated from teenage jargon to downright unladylike utterances. I found the use of one particular word very offensive. I had no idea that my little angel girl with the lovely, innocent hazel eyes had such words in her vocabulary and was using them liberally on the Internet. What would people—our friends, her peers at school, her teachers or a college admission officer—think if they were to read some of what she had written?

Without a second thought, I wrote the administrators of the site, asserted my rights of ownership to my minor child and asked that her blog be shut down immediately. Compliance was swift. Within minutes, it was down.

I picked her up on my way home from work later that day as usual. She hopped in beside me and breezily began to update me about her day at school. I responded in turn, trying to prolong the inevitable—telling her that her blog was no more, and by extension, that I knew it existed and had been monitoring it all along. Despite my certainty that I had acted correctly, I rationalized my actions to myself. For example, if she had been putting her thoughts out there for the world to see, then it was in order for me to read it too, right? After all, there is no such thing as privacy in cyberspace. If she was old enough to be online, she should know that.

Still, deep in thought, I shut out her chatter. Correspondingly, she fell quiet, and we drove in silence for a few minutes.

"I shut down your blog," I said finally, in an even tone. My voice was not angry—just the one I used when I would not tolerate any argument.

"Okay," she said cautiously.

"I shut it down because I did not like some of what you wrote," I said, citing an example. "You must know by now that what you put out there never goes away. It could come back to haunt you at the worst time— long after you are grown—long after you have forgotten about it."

"I know," she said with disarming humility.

"You always have to be careful with media," I said. "It's always very seductive, and the Internet is the most seductive of all. It's right there at your fingertips—so, so very easy. But it can make you or break you, and you have to understand that now."

"Actually, I am more ashamed that you saw what I wrote," she said. "My parents are not supposed to see that stuff."

"Let that be the least of your worries," I said. "But let this be a lesson for the rest of your life. The media are powerful beyond your ability to understand. You don't want to put anything out there unless you want the whole world to know. Moreover, once you put it out there, you can never truly take it back. That's the worst part."

"I understand, Mommy."

"Okay, Baby" I said. "I am glad because that is why I shut down your blog."

NINETEEN

It Never Rained On Christmas Day

*What is Christmas? It is tenderness for the past, courage for the present,
hope for the future. It is a fervent wish that every cup may overflow with
blessings rich and eternal, and that every path may lead to peace.*

—Agnes M. Pharo

When I was a little girl, the period between one Christmas and the next seemed like forever. Now, with the passage of time, they seem that much closer together. Just like birthdays, each Christmas is a powerful reminder of the existential fact of my mortality. But I do not mind at all because I love Christmas and the joys and good feelings that come with it.

Christmas Eve 2001, I stood inside Michaels, an arts and crafts store in Aspen Hill, Maryland, looking at the plethora of silk wreaths and artificial trees and watching my friend, Sydna, grab frantically at one item or another. She was trying desperately, it seemed, to fill her shopping cart and to reach the checkout line before closing time. After all, this was not Jamaica. There would be no Grand Market with shopping beginning at sunrise Christmas Eve and ending near dawn on Christmas morning. This was America. Soon a voice would come over the loudspeaker warning that the store would be closing in thirty minutes.

My amusement at Sydna's frantic grasping soon gave way to sadness. I realized that what I was watching was not a childish delight in the Christmas spirit or even purposeful shopping but a compulsion—a compulsion to amass more and more things that would end up stuffed in cupboards and little dark corners in a basement, never to be seen again unless they re-emerge at a yard sale, five or ten years down the road. It was an attempt to fill an empty life. But how many silk wreaths could it possibly take to fill the holes of a stunted adulthood? How many more would it take to make up for unfulfilled dreams, broken promises and the absence of real and lasting love in one's life? How many pieces of plastic could it possibly take to make Christmas happy when Christ is nowhere in the picture?

The split screen came up in my mind with delightful images of Christmases past. We had no silk wreaths or precious little stuff of any kind in rural Jamaica where I grew up. But our Christmases were always filled with warmth, gratitude and goodwill and they are among my fondest memories.

By around age six or seven, I had solved the mystery of Santa Claus. Before that, he came in under the doorways at Christmas time as we had no chimneys for him to come down. As gifts, my sisters and I would get little white dolls with yellow hair, and my brothers, little plastic trucks or cars.

For a while, I did not understand why my parents let us believe that a big, jolly fellow in a red suit sneaked under our door while we slept and put packages in pillowcases hung behind the door. Now I do understand and I am glad they did. They wanted to create romance and memories amidst the hardships of our lives and give meaning to childhood separate and apart from the tedium and difficulties of everyday life. Christmas and Santa Claus, allowed them—if only for a brief while—to make fairy tales of the drudgery of their lives as much as ours.

Of course, the Santa story is so improbable, the mystique necessarily cannot last for very long. Happily, the pain of putting him to bed, of accepting that it was as fanciful as any other fairy tale, was immediately replaced by a magic that was entirely real and no less delightful—the joy of waking up to a world seemingly always drenched in sunshine and full of family, love and laughter. God, it seemed, was always careful to make Christmas consummately sublime. Back then, it never rained on Christmas Day, or so it seemed to me.

The Christmases of my childhood meant waking up to the fragrance of my grandmother's coffee from across the street. The smell of the rich black beverage was mixed with the scent of the newly minted goat's liver and green bananas that my mother cooked for breakfast and the smell of the goat's head roasting on charcoal in the yard outside, for the soup on Boxing Day.

Christmas was waking up to stones and trees painted white in honor of the Christ child.

Christmas was waking up to the laughter of my playmates, showing off the cheap toys that their parents, like mine, had saved all year to buy.

Christmas was eating Mamma's rice and curried goat, grandmother's chicken and gungo peas, Auntie's potato pudding and soursop juice, all in the same day.

Christmas was sorrel, rum punch and ginger beer in the house all at once.

Christmas was waking up before dawn to greet the day, while the sky was still gently dark from the peace of a passing night.

Christmas was the sound of the church choir serenading daybreak with a burst of song:

> *Sing Christmas songs poinsettias red*
> *For in a lo-ow-ly manger's bed*
> *A little babe was born.*

—w—

Amidst the plastic inside Michaels, I had an epiphany—a lesson to teach my children. In case I had been remiss in driving it home before, I had to let them know that material possessions did not equal happiness; that meaning, purpose, or fulfillment cannot be bought from a department store. Nor could these things be found in silk wreaths, plastic toys, new jeans, gold, pearls, diamonds, big houses or fancy cars.

For many of us, finding meaning in life is elusive. In fact, I sometime think that the search for a purpose in life is the purpose of life. To a lesser or greater extent, meaning is found in a commitment to a way of being that honors our humanity and that of others, expressed in the quality of our sharing and caring, particularly for the less fortunate, and in our faith and hope for a future beyond our physical existence.

I had to remind Alya and Ilsa too of what Christmas means to Christians—the commemoration of the birth of the Christ Child, which, in its unfolding, was a call to sacrifice, simplicity, humility, courage, love, peace and purity.

I took immediate leave of Sydna.

No, I had to leave right this minute.

No, I did not need anything, after all.

No, I did not need a ride back.

My answers to Sydna's questions were terse. The decision to leave was not anything I could explain without hurting her feelings, and anyway she was among a few of my friends who thought I was a little weird. I did not mind that my sudden, unexplained departure could be used as further proof.

I left the store walking briskly to ward off the December chill and gave only a passing glance at the Home Depot across Connecticut Avenue. I had intended to stop there to buy two pots of poinsettias— to satisfy my longing for a tropical Christmas in cold, cold Maryland. Suddenly, it was not worth the walk.

"Mooommy!"

Alya and Ilsa abandoned the television and threw themselves at me like two excited puppies as soon as I opened the door. I savored the feeling of being wrapped in both their arms and in their unconditional love.

"Grab your hats and coats," I said, hugging them back. "We are going out."

"Where are we going?"

"Church," I said. "St. Andrews."

St. Andrew Lutheran Church was at the entrance of our apartment complex. We had never been there before, but I read the notice board as I walked by each day and I knew there was a Christmas Eve service beginning at six o'clock. If we skipped the shower and went just as we were, we would make it.

I brushed their hair and mine as quickly as I could and we were out the door.

Just as I knew that my parents had us believe in Santa Claus as much for themselves as it was for us, I knew that evening that I needed to hear again the story of Christmas and why Christ came into the world. For my children, and myself, I needed to hear how Mary and Joseph rode into Bethlehem, not in a Rolls Royce, a chariot or a gas-guzzling Hummer, but on a humble, gentle donkey, as they prepared to give birth to the Christ child.

I needed to hear that Jesus was not born in a palace, or in a five-bedroom, four-story house, but in a stable.

I needed to hear that because the Blessed Virgin Mary was not registered for baby gifts at Target, she wrapped her son in pieces of cloth and laid him on a bed of straw with the farm animals watching. And, I needed to hear the Christmas carols of long ago:

Oh Little Town of Bethlehem
How still we see thee lie
Above the deep and dreamless sleep
The silent stars go by.

Or

Once in Royal David City
Stood a lowly cattle shed
Where a mother laid her baby

In a manger for his bed.
Mary was that Mother mild,
Jesus Christ her little child.

I wanted to hear carols sung from the pulpit, accompanied by the haunting strains of an old pipe organ.

The service was simple, elegant and beautiful. High above the pulpit, a plain wooden cross on the wall looked down on the audience, reminding us not only of his birth, but of his death and resurrection. In front was the glittering Christmas tree,[30] topped by a star. The beautifully decorated tree was a contrast to the simplicity of the cross, a gentle reminder of the conversions of different worlds, one spiritual and one material, and how easy it is to confuse the two.

We shared hot chocolate and cookies with the congregation afterward to cap an evening poignant in its simplicity and in the power of the message of Jesus' birth:

Glory to God in the highest, and on earth peace, goodwill toward men.

—m—

"**D**id you enjoy the service?" I asked on the short walk back to our apartment.

"Yes," they agreed. "We must go more often."

"Good," I said. "Can we make a pact too?"

"What?"

"That as of this day, wherever in the world we are on Christmas Eve, whether we are together or apart, we will find ourselves in church so we can always hear the story of Jesus and remind ourselves of how and why Jesus came."

They agreed.

We made it to St. Andrew's four years in a row. Christmas Eve 2005, we arrived in Florida too late to find a church. We have missed a few others since, mostly for the same reason—travelling out of town and arriving too late to get to Christmas Eve service. But we have not forgotten the pact. Beyond the need to remind ourselves of the true meaning of Christmas, it has kept us out of the stores on Christmas Eve and within an atmosphere of fellowship, serenity and genuine goodwill. Our pact has also served to advance the idea of Christmas as a symbol of unconditional love, sacrifice and simplicity.

In a culture of rabid consumerism, this simple pact was also about a struggle to inspire my children to live every day of their lives true to what is real and meaningful. This way, when I am old or gone, they will not spend Christmas Eve or too much of their lives in some store, least of all one filled with plastic wreaths, desperately grasping for purpose or meaning in things and places and activities where they can never be found.

TWENTY

I Am Worthy

The flower that blooms in adversity is the rarest and most beautiful of all.

—Chinese Proverb

"I bet you are embarrassed because you have a fat child."

Alya's ready smile and gentle nature belie a tough, unrelenting spirit. As incongruous as it sounds, it took me a while to realize that her innate gentleness was not in conflict with her strength. I say this because I should have known better. In fact, I have said the same thing often enough about myself—how easily some seem to mistake my quiet, compassionate and non-confrontational side for weakness. Yet, here I was doing the same thing to my daughter—assuming that because she was gentle and sweet natured she was less equipped to confront life's many challenges, including those we face as a family.

Over time, I learned. Alya was unafraid to challenge anything or anyone if she felt her cause was worth fighting for. The realization brought a flood of tenderness and respect for her, as I watched her evolution from childhood into blossoming womanhood. It was rewarding to see my child demonstrate her ability to make her own way in a dog-eat-dog world and it didn't matter that her toughness now was directed squarely at me. Secretly, I applauded it.

Still, the tears running down her face filled my heart with sadness, despair, shame, and anxiety, even as I tried to reassure her that my concern about her weight had nothing to do with embarrassment. After all, I was not given to too much vanity myself and I knew that my firstborn—the person, who more than anyone else, fuelled my ability to love with power, intensity, purity and selflessness—was far more than her weight or her appearance. But I was worried about her health and the extent to which society would fail to look past the external to see the beauty of the soul within.

My concern was not misplaced. My instinct, and research into prevailing medical opinions in an attempt to manage my own chronic medical condition better, convince me that the quality of life for overweight children is often compromised. They are at risk for pediatric hypertension, type 2 diabetes, heart disease and orthopedic problems caused by too much stress on the weight-bearing joints. I was also concerned about how my daughter might see herself in a society that places high premium on appearance and how that would impact her relationships since overweight people are often marginalized by their peers. Psychologists say the feeling of being an outcast is among the most critical problems that obese children face.

From what Alya was saying, I was not handling my concern very well. Instead, my responses were exacerbating the problem. I was making her feel badly about her weight and achieving something different from what I intended.

I thought of how much I have always loved her—from that day, four months into conception, when I felt the quickening, the first tiny flutter in my stomach confirming that a living, breathing being was growing there—bone of my bone, flesh of my flesh. I thought of her too as a chubby, pink-cheeked newborn; a happy, smiling toddler; and a placid easygoing young girl. Surely, greater love has no mother than this, I thought.

Now, a pre-teen, Alya was delightful, pleasing and lovely in all the ways that mattered. How then could I treat her in a way that would make her feel less valuable, less lovely inside?

Yet, I knew that she was right to question how I was dealing with her weight. I knew because I often questioned myself on whether I was doing a good enough job of balancing my concern for her with gentleness and sensitivity to a difficult situation for both of us, but more so for her. I knew because I was always watching her, watching how much she ate, and reminding her to do her exercise—to use the exercise equipment that I bought to make it easier.

The stationary bike came first. Alya barely spared it a passing glance and eventually I moved it from our tiny living room to the balcony. Then came the expensive treadmill from Sears, which I planted squarely in front of the television in the living room.

Nothing happened.

In the meantime, she had gone from overweight to being obese, meaning that fat accounted for more than twenty-five percent of her body weight. I searched frantically for the reasons her weight had ballooned. Lack of physical activity, poor eating habits, socioeconomic status, and underlying hereditary physiological conditions such as thyroid disease, are the most commonly identified causes of childhood obesity.

Researchers say excessive television watching—which expends little energy and is normally done while consuming high-calorie snacks such as potato chips—also contributes to obesity among young children and adolescents. Children with two obese parents are also at a higher risk either due to hereditary factors or modeling attitudes to food and exercise. Finally, the research says, infants born to overweight mothers are likely to gain more weight by age three months than children born to mothers of normal weight. I began to see how some of those factors manifested themselves in our lives.

I was thin all my life until I became pregnant with Alya. Unprepared for what turned out to be a difficult pregnancy, I ate far more than usual. Worse, I ate and drank with little discipline, sticking only to the foods I tolerated easily: eggnog and chocolate milk and other dairy-based foods. I gained more than fifty pounds, and gave birth to a baby weighing almost nine pounds.

Alya grew into a chubby toddler. Although I kept a wary eye on her weight, I was not worried, as obesity did not run in my family. In time, I believed, she would shed the "baby fat." Besides, she was a happy-go-lucky kid who enjoyed playing on the monkey bars, rollerblading, riding her bike and playing in the swimming pool. And I rarely allowed her to eat junk food.

She did not shed the excess weight. Rather, as we transitioned through stressful periods, she gained more. The more she gained, the more frantic I became. My daughter had become an unfavorable statistic—an obese child.

I wanted Alya to exercise more and eat less. I would do anything that would help her shed the pounds and give me back my little girl before it was too late. My anxiety ran amok sometimes and I turned on her, scolding her and begging her to help me help her.

There was constant talk in the media about the obesity epidemic among young children and adolescents in America. More than a quarter of obese adults were overweight children—a situation that placed them at higher risk for developing more severe health problems later in life. My daughter, I learned, was part of the fifteen percent of obese children and adolescents and in a high-risk category. Overall, between five and seven percent of black children are considered obese.

I did not need statistics or media buzz to convince me of the risks Alya faced. In 1997, six years after the birth of my two children, I had not lost the sixty pounds that I gained during the pregnancies. I suffered my first health crisis then and found myself on an unscheduled trip to the emergency room. A routine visit to the doctor turned up extremely high levels of sugar in my blood. Further tests revealed equally high levels of cholesterol. As a precaution, the doctor sent me to the emergency room to begin steps to bring down the levels of sugar and cholesterol levels. Long before the lab confirmed it, I was feeling all that the test results said: my body was disintegrating. Excess fatigue and insomnia were among the symptoms I was experiencing.

Initially, the diagnosis that I was "sick" made matters worse. It deepened my anxiety about my life and my two toddlers: Will I live to see them grow up? What if I don't? What would their lives be like growing up without a mother? What would people tell them about me? How did I get to a point where I seemed on the verge of denying my children all that I had to offer them as their mother? I knew and I had to heal. I had to see them through.

Alya, in the meantime, was absorbing much of my anxiety and found her solace in food. It was not hard to figure out. In those evenings when she was home alone, she had ample time to eat more than she should. I soon learned that I had to do more than avoid McDonald's and all the other fast food outlets to help control her weight.

"Its not that I eat bad food," she told our family doctor candidly at one of our office visits. "It's just that I eat too much of whatever there is."

At age ten, she had her first medical emergency—a dislocated hip that began simply with an uneven gait that she could not explain. An X-ray taken about two weeks after I first noticed her limp revealed the dislocation. The doctor at Holy Cross Hospital explained that her body was growing too big and too fast for her bones. Under pressure, the hip joint had simply given way and would have to be surgically corrected. Heartsick, I sat in the hospital lounge a few days later and watched the doctors wheel her away in operating room gown and cap.

When the surgery was over, Dr. Maurice Cates, the surgeon in charge, had a warning for me: the other hip would be at risk if she gained any more weight, or even if she remained at her current weight. He insisted that it was my responsibility to correct because she was not in charge. It was now or never. I had to get her weight and her eating habits under control before it was too late—before she went off college where she would have free reign to eat whatever and however much she wanted to.

—⁓—

Life is never cut and dried. It does not unfold in a straight line and there are no easy solutions to some of the challenges that we are confronted with. Losing weight as an adult is hard; getting a child to lose weight is harder. It is not nearly as simple as recognizing symptoms, obtaining a diagnosis and proceeding to a treatment plan.

Between any of those steps, there are any numbers of intervening factors, some of which are beyond our control.   In spite of the many things outside of my control, I agreed with Dr. Cates and I believed then as I do now that I failed my daughter in very important ways. I should have maintained better control over the factors that led to her weight ballooning out of control. I should have been more careful about her weight from the time she was born and that care should have continued through infancy and childhood. I should have fed her far more slices of oranges and mangoes and less store-bought products; more water and natural fruit juices than juice concentrates; more steamed cabbage and broccoli than rice. And, I should have paid greater attention to my post-partum practices before they became lifetime habits.

Experts say, for example, that exclusive breastfeeding for a minimum of three months is a good safeguard against weight gain for children and more so if it is continued, along with other foods, for the child's first year. Recognition of signals of satiety and delayed introduction of solid foods are also good measures in infancy that should be combined with proper nutrition to prevent excess weight gain. Selections of low-fat snacks, promoting physical activity and, by extension, reducing television viewing and other sedentary activities, are essential during the toddler years and beyond.

Now that Alya was older, dealing with her weight would be far more difficult. Whatever I did, or tried to do, needed her cooperation, and despite her recognition that there was a problem, that did not mean she was ready or willing to follow her doctor's order to exercise more, control portion size and avoid foods laden with sugar, trans fat and empty calories. Most experts agree that a combination of these efforts would ultimately yield results. Behavior modification, including self-monitoring, recording food intake, eating slowly, limiting and using rewards and incentives for desirable behaviors were good practices as well.

Despite the challenges, helping Alya at home was relatively easy. At least I had control over what came into the house and as long as I was there, over how much she ate. It was a different story at school. I visited her during lunch time one day to see exactly what she was eating.

It turned out to be the worst of what the cafeteria had to offer—French fries, cupcakes, and potato chips. I went to the cafeteria manager and requested she be disallowed from purchasing any of those foods without my written permission.

What an excruciatingly difficult place for a mother to be in —torn between the need to help her child and the fear that she might interpret it to mean that there was something wrong with her because of her weight. Worst, what a painful place for a young girl—called upon to exercise tremendous discipline in an area where millions of adults fail every day!

I did my best and I worried—silently mostly, openly sometimes. More and more, I saw her facing increased risk to her health including heart disease, cancer, diabetes and high cholesterol, conditions which some physicians say can have their genesis in childhood obesity. Aortic fatty streaks, the first stages of atherosclerosis—or hardening of the arteries—can also begin in childhood. Further, recent statistics show an alarming increase in non-insulin dependent diabetes among children and adolescents, a condition with many potential complications and the increased risk of a shortened life span.

I worried too about her psychological and social well-being and the likelihood of her being lonely and alienated as she grew older. It does not take much to recognize that in America, people do not like fat—or fat people. Indeed, media images of what the typical, attractive female form is supposed to be not only deplore the idea of people above a certain size; it perpetuates standards that are unrealistic for people outside of Hollywood. Being significantly overweight clearly puts one in a category below that of normal people.

I hated the thought that anyone would look at my beautiful child this way. In my attempt to make sure that it did not happen, I sometimes felt like I was looking at her in exactly the same way. She felt it, and challenged me on it.

—m—

I bet you are embarrassed because you have a fat child.

She got through elementary school, and suffered through junior high. Through it all, she had a small core of friends who knew and loved her sweetness. Although she was still significantly overweight by the time she reached high school, increasingly, it seemed to matter less and less. Suddenly, the bright shining light that she is was streaming through. Her circle of friends expanded as she gave in to her natural ability to lead and her desire to explore the world. Once again, she was the happy-go-lucky young girl I used to know.

I relaxed considerably.

One morning as I checked my fasting glucose to make sure my sugar was fine, she stuck out her finger and asked me to check hers as well just to make sure. It was perfect—near the lower end of normal. Although she is yet to completely conquer her weight problem, I have no doubts that in time she will. The vegetarian diet she has adopted is beginning to yield noticeable results. Furthermore, I know now that anyone with the character to do and achieve as much as she has, also has the willpower to overcome excess weight as soon as she is ready.

Just now, she stuck her head around the doorway as I worked at the computer.

"I am going for a walk, Mommy," she said.

"Go, Baby," I said. "Go!"

TWENTY-ONE

Of Perfect Love

May you never take one single breath for granted
God forbid love ever leave you empty handed...
And when you get the choice to sit it out or dance
I hope you dance

—Lee Ann Womack

"Did you have me out of wedlock?"

I knew the question would come some day, but I did not expect it so soon. Alya was barely five years old. It never occurred to me that at that age children thought about those things, especially since her father and I lived together like a married couple. Who would know that we had not said our vows in front of a minister or signed a piece of paper in front of a marriage officer? As far as I was concerned, my unmarried state was just my "dirty" little secret that my babies were oblivious to.

The day she came home from school and charged at me came as a surprise. Worse, was the hurt look in her eyes.

"How could you Mommy?" she asked. "How could you?"

It was my moment of deepest shame. Not only was I being put on trial by my five-year-old, but her question brought to the surface my profound sense of disappointment in myself. It reminded me just how far I had strayed from my ideals, which included having children only in the context of a happy marriage.

When I became an unwed mother, I rationalized it. It was nearing the end of the 20th century and I was far from being alone, I told myself. Millions of women in the United States and around the world, for different reasons, have chosen to have children outside of wedlock. In fact, out-of-wedlock births in the United States have been increasing since around 1970, accelerating in the 1990s and reaching an all-time high of more than one and a half million—or four in ten babies—in 2005. In Jamaica, my home country, approximately seventy percent of children are born out of wedlock. Based on those numbers, I had not done anything unusual; there was no need for either shame or embarrassment.

The truth is, though, I was not okay with having my children out of wedlock or in having them numbered among those statistics. It was never what I wanted for my children or myself. By my own standard, therefore, I had fallen short, which was infinitely more difficult to accept than falling short of someone else's expectations.

—◊◊◊—

I grew up in a poor but secure home with two parents linked by the sacred promise of "for better or worse, till death us do part." In spite of what seemed like unending hardship, they have stuck to that commitment. Their life together was neither always good, nor always happy, but I remember more good days than bad ones.

Even in the worst of times, I never once felt that either parent was going anywhere. I never feared that my parents would divorce and split up our family, and I never felt that I was not part of a unit that was strong and unshakeable. Always, I felt like I was a part of a metaphysical connection—that my parents belonged together and their children belonged within their union.

Ultimately, I had a very good example of what marriage was supposed to be—love, loyalty, devotion, commitment and a safe harbor from the storms of life for adults and children alike. The sense of security that I experienced as a child gave me the confidence I needed to venture into the world in pursuit of my dreams. I always knew that if things did not work out, I could go home to people who would always love and support me. My parents, the security of home and the constancy and love of family, were my soft place to fall. I wanted the same for my children and more.

As a young girl my dreams came true over and over again—in my mind. I dreamt of an even better marriage for myself—a partnership where I would not be sentenced to child rearing, cooking and housecleaning for the rest of my life. Rather, I would develop my full potential as a woman and human being, thereby enhancing my core role as wife and mother, rather than detract from it. In addition, I imagined a greater sense of material well-being emerging out of a union that was open, honest, productive and fostered a consistent atmosphere of mutual respect, caring and unselfish love.

Doing better than my mother would be easy, as far as I was concerned. Already, I was better educated than she was; I had earned more money in the first year of my career than she had ever done in her lifetime. I would not have to prepare dinner over a brushwood fire or a charcoal stove as she had done throughout much of my childhood. Nor would I have to skin my knees scrubbing the floor with cloth and pail. I would not have to carry buckets of water on my head over long distances for domestic use, and I would not have to curve my legs around a big aluminum pan to scrub clothes, stained with red dirt, until my hands were shriveled and blistered. With so many advantages, I believed I was poised to be a wonderful homemaker and to enjoy the rewards of a long and happy marriage.

As I envisioned it, married life would begin with a wonderfully romantic ceremony in a special chapel where I would commit to my finest ideals—loyalty, fidelity, devotion, caring and compassion. I would say my vows in front of my most cherished friends and family. I had even picked out the chapel—on the Campus of the University of the West Indies at Mona in Jamaica. Its stark sturdiness had an abiding appeal for me, not just because of what it was, but what it symbolized—simplicity, elegance, endurance and more than anything else, transformation.

—m—

The structure that is now the chapel at Mona began in 1799 on the Gale's Valley Estate in Trelawny, halfway across the island. After more than a century and a half as a rum distillery, the building fell into disuse. The late Princess Alice, Countess of Athlone and chancellor of what was then the University College of the West Indies, took the unusual step of asking the owner for the building which she believed would make a great chapel for the island's first university and where, as well, its Georgian beauty could be better preserved. The owner agreed, and in 1956 the building was transported, stone by stone, from the old estate to its present location, near the entrance of the campus. London architects Norman & Dawbarn supervised the reconstruction, taking great care to preserve its original Georgian style. It was officially dedicated on February 14, 1960.

I admired the lovely old building, but more than that, I found the idea of building a chapel out of a rum distillery infinitely appealing. Rum is heavily abused in Jamaica and its overuse manifested in all kinds of anti-social behavior. Therefore, taking a rum distillery and remaking it into a chapel was, for me, a symbol of enduring hope that something worthwhile, beautiful and wholesome can come out of the most challenging situations. In my mind, marriage—the union of two different lives together—was a little like that.

Square and solid, the chapel looked like a safe place to be in a storm, its austerity softened by the immaculately kept garden filled with all the tropical blossoms of my childhood. To the east, the smoky mountain peaks, with their countless grooves and ridges, are constant reminders that life too is a series of valleys and peaks. They are reminders too that, on our human journeys, it is from this variety and endurance come wisdom—the arrival at a place of consummate understanding about our place in the world and our ability to accept with equanimity that life is both good and bad and that real joy means embracing it all.

—⟋⟍—

I never had my wedding in the chapel—never had a wedding at all even though my relationship with the father of my children had all the appearances of a marriage, even a happy one at times. Appearances, however, are not the foundation upon which to build a lifelong commitment, and I refused to live my life being true to appearances without the requisite substance. Unwed motherhood for me, then, was not about the fear of losing my freedom as a strong-willed woman, nor was it about any kind of disregard for the institution of marriage. On the contrary, it was more about the esteem in which I held the institution and the fear that I would not have been able to keep the vow—till death do us part.

Unlike the commitment explicit in a marriage, having children does not warrant a declaration before man and God to yoke one's life to another person's. Instead, the commitment implicit in motherhood is based on the fact that my children are the seeds of my body and eternally and irrevocably mine. It was far easier for me to have them than to commit to marriage.

—⟋⟍—

Although it is no longer the social taboo that it used to be, the increasing number of children born out of wedlock is cause for concern. Studies have shown that African-American children, for example, were more likely to grow up living with both parents during slavery than they are today.[31] Children being raised by only one parent—in most cases the mother—are at higher risk of being delinquent than their counterparts born and raised in stable, two-parent homes. Two-parent families are more likely to have greater financial security, less dislocation and a shared workload, including child supervision.

Single-parent families, meanwhile, are more likely to experience the opposite. Most of these families are headed by women, who typically earn less than men. As a result, most children of single-parent families live in poverty. The financial difficulties, combined with the demands of taking care of children alone, is often overwhelming for most women, despite their best efforts. It is for these reasons that many people view single parenthood as a harbinger for undesirable outcomes for the children involved. These include underperformance in school and delinquent behaviors such as teenage pregnancy, drug use and truancy. Data shows that expectations of negative outcomes for children of single-parent families are well founded. For example, seventy-two percent of teenage murderers and sixty percent of those committing sex crimes are from single-parent homes. Overall, children from single-parent homes are eleven times more likely to exhibit violent behavior.

Conscious of this bleak outlook, I have sheltered and protected my children to the point of being paranoid at times. I have shielded them from these expected negative outcomes of their status as children raised by a single parent, as well as from any possible notion that they are any less wanted, loved or valued. So far, they seem to be sailing on just fine—overachieving in many ways and adjusting well emotionally and socially.

Nonetheless, I hope that neither unwed motherhood nor single parenthood will ever be a reality for Alya and Ilsa.

I hope that they will learn their lessons in life not merely by emulating the things I have done right but by avoiding those things that I have done than are less than desirable.

I hope sincerely that, in the course of their lives, they will each be able to realize the union of their souls with that of a man who values them, and who they value and respect in turn.

Ultimately, I hope they will have the opportunity to wear their favorite dresses, to sing their favorite songs, and to make their life-long commitments surrounded by people who have always loved them unconditionally. More than anything, I hope my daughters will find true love— as strong, as bright and as enduring as a tropical sun.

TWENTY-TWO

Perfect As We Are

Great love and great achievements involve great risk.

—Anonymous

The train snaked its way into the station at Fort Lauderdale, Florida. Barely able to hear the operator's voice above the babble of passengers heading for South Beach, we almost missed the stop. I scrambled off just in time, behind Alya and Ilsa.

For a moment, I wished that I was headed to the big party at South Beach. Tomorrow was New Year's Day—my birthday. Maybe just for once, I could be someone else. Maybe I could let my hair down and shake my booty all night long.

I laughed at my thoughts. Me shaking my booty all night long? Fidel Castro in the White House? The two Saturday morning Jehovah's Witnesses praying on my doorstep?

Highly unlikely.

Outside in the sunshine, we hailed a cab and directed the driver to my sister's apartment in Lauderhill. The driver was a handsome man with a sonorous voice and a charming accent I failed to pinpoint.

"So where are you from?" I asked, as soon as we settled down.

"Haiti. I am from Haiti," he answered, taking his eyes off the road and turning to favor me with a happy grin—as if he wanted a medal for being from the poorest nation in the Western Hemisphere.

I should have known, I thought. That compelling mix of cadences could only be Haitian—some French, a little West African and an abundance of Caribbean rhythms.

"How long have you been here?"

"Fifteen years. Fifteen loooong years," he sang.

"Sounds like you are ready to go home," I laughed.

"Ready?" he asked, his brows climbing up to his forehead. "Been ready to go home since the day I set foot in this country."

"Why don't you go back then?"

"Nothing there to go home to. Nothing. Haiti is a mess, you know that. At least here you can drive a doggone cab. You can make a living. There's nothing in Haiti for me."

"Do you have family there?"

"Yea, my old folks are there. They are there. Went back two years ago. So where you from?"

"Jamaica," I delivered, rivaling him in pride of ownership—as if I wanted a medal just because I came out of the most delightfully complex and fractious island of the archipelago.

"Jaamaicaaa!" he echoed. "Beautiful island woman from Jaamaicaaaa! How long you been here?"

He took his eyes off the road again.

"Two years," I answered. "I have been here two years."

Already, I was copying his habit of saying everything twice. Was that a Haitian thing?

I did not meet too many Haitians in Maryland, and although Haiti was only a hundred and twenty miles northeast of Jamaica, there was limited interaction between the two nations partly because of the former's history of political instability, non-existent or unreliable transportation, and the different languages spoken—French and French-based Creole in Haiti and English and English-based Creole in Jamaica. Even so, a quiet bond resonates between the two nations, forged by their common history as people of African descent. Further, since Jamaicans take their reputation as rebels seriously, they have an abiding admiration for the Haitian people—the first in the Western

Hemisphere to fight off the yoke of slavery. This makes them the ultimate rebels.

My Haitian brother interrupted my thoughts.

"Why did you come here beautiful woman from Jamaica?"

"To go to school."

"Will you go back?"

"I want to."

"Well, Jamaica is not as bad as Haiti, eh? You are lucky with that. You can go back when you feel like."

"I get what you are saying. Haiti does seem like a basket case sometimes, but Jamaica is screwed up in many ways too. It's not all like the tourist board commercials you see on TV. "

"Baby, the whole Third World is screwed up. All of Africa is screwed up. South America is screwed up. The Caribbean is screwed up—some more than some. It's screwed up because our leaders are corrupt. The businessmen come from abroad and take what we have and we don't even realize. I tell you, we all got it bad. That's why we are all refugees in America. But at least in Jamaica, you have, you know, political security...stability, I mean."

"That's one of the good things we have going for us, I suppose," I responded. "If we lose that we are done, and sometimes I fear it's just a matter of time. In the meantime, the economy is not growing, inflation is way too high, there are not enough jobs and people kill people for sport down there. We have to find a way to make that stability work for us. To transfer, ahmm, translate it into something more meaningful than what we have done so far."

"I hear you Sistah. I hear you. But we can't give up, you know. We have to hope. Haiti's been struggling for a long time, but still, we can't give up. It's all we've got. My spirit is bound to Haiti forever just like your spirit is bound to Jamaica. So we have to hope. We must hope."

"Yes, hope. We must hope."

I turned the words over in my head.

Hope.

It is a good word. It was what spurred the Haitian leader, Toussaint L'Overture, to lead a revolution and a whole nation to freedom. It is why today, even though many Haitians still have so little, they can still stand tall, unbent and unbowed. It is why I left my own land to come to America, and why, buffeted by one storm or another, I have stayed put.

Hope for tomorrow.

Hope for my children.

So often it seems that hope is all we have.

The driver pulled up outside the apartment. Effortlessly, he took our suitcases in both hands and walked with them to the elevator. At the top, I tipped him more generously than I could afford—a *bon jour* and *adieu*—because I knew it would be my only meeting with this charming man driving a cab for a living, even though our roots were so deeply connected.

"What's your name?" he asked.

"Grace." I said. "And yours?"

"Michael," he said. "Michael."

"Well Michael, have a wonderful New Year."

"You too, beautiful island woman from Jamaica. You too."

He gave me his sunshine grin and then he was gone, walking with the rhythmic grace of a man with the sounds of the drums in his head, the passions of the hot lands in his blood.

I wished there was a way I could see him again, but just as quickly I dismissed the thought. He was gone and within minutes he would be back on the road, lost among the hundreds of immigrants driving yellow taxis in South Florida. Besides, in a day or two, I would be back up North, caring for my children, and not particularly concerned about Michael or any other man.

—⁂—

This absence of male companionship is a reality for many single women, who, consumed with the responsibility of raising their children, forego the pleasures or the headaches. Many of us simply do not have enough time and enough emotional and spiritual energy to both parent and give to a partner. For most of us, our children necessarily come first. Most well-thinking mothers are unwilling to add dating to our lives or risk parading too many strangers through their children's. The drawbacks do not compensate for the advantages. I got used to going it alone.

I cast one last look at Michael's strong shoulders. So what if he drove a cab for a living? It was honest work. Plus, he was a fine specimen of manhood; big and handsome, bright and engaging and he had flirted so beautifully that neither of my girls could have picked up on the energy in the car.

Or so I thought.

Alya promptly took a seat opposite me as soon as I dropped my bag and sat on my sister's beige leather couch.

"Mommy?"

It was barely a question. I looked up from unbuckling my sandals to see her brown eyes sparkling more impishly than usual.

"Would you like a companion?"

For once, I truly did not know. I had not thought it through carefully, perhaps because I had no real reason to, or because I was accepting my life just the way it was: a single black mother in her mid-thirties, part-time worker and full-time graduate student. These variables represent a multiplicity of issues—most of which did not lend themselves to meeting a prospective companion and sustaining a steady relationship.

As a single mother, I am nearly always with my children. Apart from those moments when I sorely longed for a break, I did not mind. The girls were energetic and fun to be with, and it was my sacred duty as a mother to care for and to protect them.

Conventional wisdom says that the chances of a woman in her mid-thirties meeting viable male partners diminish by the year. For example, most black men in my age group are already married. Those who are not are incarcerated, assumed to be either gay or HIV positive, not looking to be involved with a woman with children, seriously committed to bachelorhood or divorced with loads of baggage.

As a black woman, a dark-skinned one at that, I am not necessarily the first choice of candidates for companionship. Stereotypes of the neck-shaking, finger-pointing, snarling, angry black woman abound. More and more, the "strong black woman" seems to be public enemy number one—an obnoxious being to be avoided at best, feared at worst. Not only is she unworthy and undeserving of love and attention, but she has reached a level of "unfemaleness" where she can live without her softer side. In reality, the "strong black woman" is one who has decided that she will not sell herself short; she will do whatever it takes to take care of herself and her children, including bludgeoning a few male egos if they get in the way.

As an educated black woman, I am in an even more awkward position: competing for the limited number of educated, straight, free and functional black men, or marrying "down"—to someone less accomplished by society's standards. Someone like Michael, for example.

Fortunately, I learned early on not to confuse a man's worth with his occupation or job title, substance with appearance, or degrees with real education. By extension, I learned that character is important. If he is a man of character, in my eyes, it wouldn't matter if he were a plumber, a priest or a cab driver.

Then, there was the natural reticence about bringing a strange man into my daughters' lives. I had to be careful about their safety and about the example I was setting for them. Sometimes though, even as a brief respite from my daily routine, I longed for pleasant male companionship. Tall, dark, attractive and quintessentially Caribbean, Michael appealed to that need.

For once, I did not feel like having a long conversation with Alya or to explain the laws of immediate attraction to her. I chose to answer her question with one of my own.

"Why would you ask me that?"

"Umm. I just wondered," she answered, her eyes still twinkling.

"Okay," I said. "Well, then would you mind if I did have a companion?"

"Of course," she returned promptly, unapologetically. "Our life is perfect just the way it is. You, my sister and me. I don't want anybody else in our house."

So, there. It was done.

Seven years later, Ilsa, my younger daughter, would revisit the issue.

"Do you feel like you are missing out on something because you don't have a man?" she asked abruptly one day as we drove home from the mall. This time I could answer honestly, frankly and without too much thought. It was shortly after I had bought my house and enlisted the help of a contractor for some minor renovations. The three bedrooms, and the master bathroom, I had painted myself. The children picked out the colors for their room and I picked what I wanted for mine. There were no conflicts, just a wonderful sense of equilibrium and satisfaction.

"Not really," I said slowly. "Most of the times I actually enjoy being single."

I reeled off the advantages.

"My life is less complicated this way. I am an autonomous person; I get to make my own decisions, big or small, without having to negotiate, and I don't have to clean up after anyone."

I sighed at the disadvantages.

"But there are times when I am deeply lonely. Times when I would really like to share my life with someone—you know someone to go to the movies or to dinner with, or for a walk in the woods, just to have an adult conversation with. Married or single, Baby Dear, it's a huge trade-off."

So would I like a companion?

Maybe. If he is fully grown, well-evolved and genuinely liberated.

TWENTY-THREE

Spare The Rod

When you make a mistake, don't look back at it long. Take the reason of the thing into your mind, and then look forward. Mistakes are lessons of wisdom. The past cannot be changed. The future is yet in your power.

—Phyllis Bottome

I went after my daughters down a store aisle for the umpteenth time in less than an hour. They were not minding me at all and at ages five and seven, I thought they were old enough to understand the rules we had gone over so many times: they were not supposed to randomly touch or pick up things that did not belong to them; they were not supposed to constantly run up and down the store aisle as if they were on the playground, and they were not supposed to run away from me in these huge stores, the size of which we never had back home. The size of many of the stores amplified my fear of losing one of the children in the same way that I have seen in the U.S. media and covered as a journalist in Jamaica. I tried to keep my daughters within the range of my vision as much as possible.

That day in the Aspen Hill Kmart, they ignored me completely. Every time I paused to look at something, one or the other would promptly disappear. Over and over again, I found myself walking up and down the aisles, looking under clothes racks and even heading to the restroom in search of them. What should have been a worthwhile trip to get them a few school supplies turned into an exercise in frustration. Before long, I had had enough. They needed to understand, once and for all, how I expected them to behave in public, I fumed silently.

"Okay," I told them finally. "Since you want to misbehave, just go ahead and do it as much as you want because when I get home, you are both going to get whipped."

They got it.

It was not the first time and it would not be the last. Between the ages of five and nine, I spanked them occasionally-no more than three times in a year. My standards were not arbitrary. Accidents or honest-to-goodness mistakes were never reasons for spanking. Willful disobedience, which could have resulted in harmful consequences for self or others, sometimes did. I thought it was fair and that they understood.

Recently I apologized for ever spanking them. Ilsa was matter-of-fact.

"It has made us who we are," she said thoughtfully.

I should have been happy that she took it so well, but I was not. But for their refusal to clean their rooms, they are delightful girls, bright, well-mannered and accomplished for their ages. They could have been just as wonderful without me ever causing them pain, physically or emotionally. Alya shared my view.

"It's lazy," she said. "Spanking is a lazy way to discipline a child."

"If I could change one thing about the way that I have raised you guys, it would have been that," I told her. "I hope you will do better by your own children. There is really no need to hit them and there are no humane ways of spanking, regardless of what anyone says."

—m—

To spank or not is one of those eternal debates. While many parents see spanking as both cruel and unnecessary, others believe that it is an important tool in child rearing and part of the sacred responsibility of parenting. Christian parents who interpret the Bible strictly, for example, are likely to see corporal punishment as essential to child rearing. From their perspective, they are heeding the oft-repeated expression that one should not "spare the rod and spoil the child," which many ascribe to the Holy Bible. Interestingly, I found out that it is not in the Bible at all; it was coined by British poet and satirist, Samuel Butler. Still, many passages in the Bible, particularly in the book of Proverbs, seems to support corporal punishment. Chapter 13 verse 24, for example, tells us:

He that spareth his rod hateth his son: but he that loveth him chasteneth betimes.

Chapter 19, verse 18:

Chasten thy son while there is hope and let not thy soul spare for his crying.

Chapter 22, verse 15:

Folly is bound in the heart of a child, but the rod of discipline will drive it far from him.

Proverbs Chapter 23:13, 23:14 and 29:15 all give support to corporal punishment if interpreted literally. In the New Testament, support comes from texts like Hebrews 12:6-8:

For whom the Lord loveth he chasteneth, and scourgeth every son whom he receiveth. If he endureth chastening, God dealeth with you as with sons; for what son is he whom the father chasteneth not? But if ye be without chastisement, whereof all are partakers, then are ye bastards and not sons.

In Jamaica, where secular society is deeply influenced by an ever-present religious fundamentalism, the question of corporal punishment at home was hardly debated. Most people believe that it is a matter of course. The average West Indian male—even if he has never set foot in church, even if he is a rum-drinker and a philanderer—will quote the Bible to support why he believes that spanking his children is a natural part of raising them and why it is his sacred duty to administer it.

My mother was the beater in my family. I recall being spanked by my father no more than once as a child—a spanking instigated by my mother. She, meanwhile, would beat us repeatedly, particularly my older sister and me with great cruelty at times and for no obvious reasons. As an adult, I realize that she beat us out of the anguish and frustration of her life not because it was the best way.

—⚉—

I spent most of my childhood in the same home with my parents, six brothers and four sisters. My father, the mythical head of the home, was distinguished by his brilliance and his love of talk. He spent his working life first as a common laborer and then as a low-level civil servant. It was a disappointing reality because he was capable of so much more. Although he was not educated beyond the secondary level, other people with similar qualifications and less innate capabilities were able to advance far beyond what he was able to accomplish. His foibles notwithstanding, he is a man of deep integrity—a man who would never tell a lie, break a promise, disclose a secret, or steal a cracker even if he were starving. He would have been good for high office, but he obviously lacked the ambition and ruthlessness that would have allowed him more success. My mother, however, had the qualities my father lacked but she did not attain his level of education or life experience.

My parents' odd combination of capabilities and shortcomings explains in part why we spent our growing-up years in poverty, without much of life's basic necessities and the source of our next meal often in doubt. Further, even though I grew up with both parents in theory, my father was rarely ever home. He left for work early in the morning, returned long after we had gone to bed at night and slept in on weekends to catch up. For all reasonable purposes, my mother raised the eleven of us mostly alone.

As an adult, I often wonder how my mother was able to do so. As a mother of only two, I have been frustrated enough, at times, to question my ability to respond effectively to the demands of being responsible for my life and theirs. It is out of this profound appreciation of the challenges inherent in being a mother and an understanding of the particular anguish of her life that I long ago forgave my mother for the times she yelled, screamed, shouted, cursed and slapped my siblings and me, for the little errors in judgment to which every child is entitled.

Like Ilsa, I believe that there were some benefits from my mother's methods: I grew up well-disciplined and determined to walk the straight and narrow, in part out of a healthy fear of her. That would hold me in good stead as I made my way through school and navigated the challenges of my teen years. It was also good enough to help me out of the crushing poverty that was our life. What then is there to question?

I have never seriously analyzed whether the end justified the means, but I decided never to slap my children once I had them. I figured that outcome notwithstanding, I had to find a better way, which should not be too hard since there was already so much about my life that was qualitatively better than my mother's.

My education and income, for example, meant that I had a machine to wash my clothes: I did not have to sit over a big aluminum pan with a scrubbing brush for hours at a time. It meant that I had a vacuum cleaner, so my knees would not be chipped from kneeling on the hard, cold floor. It meant a kitchen with a real stove; I did not have to cook over a wood fire with the blue smoke and onions stinging my eyes with equal intensity. It meant that I had indoor plumbing; to my children, an outdoor latrine was a quaint contraption that they would never quite understand. Plus, I had two children to her eleven.

—⁊⁊—

My children were never spanked during the first five years of their lives. Things changed when I left my home country to study in the United States and my life became riddled with uncertainties and anxiety that I had not bargained for. Gone was the ready access to friends and relatives and the network of support that they provided, including those who were doctors and nurses, who I could call for advice on how to treat simple ailments. Instead, I was in a place where social isolation was real, and health insurance counted for everything.

Furthermore, I had exchanged a real paycheck for a graduate assistant's salary supplemented with a little scholarship money. For the most part, the stipend was all I had. But what if I didn't get that check, just once? More importantly, I was mostly alone with my children. What if I got sick one day and couldn't walk them to school or open the door when they got home? Tired, anxious and frustrated about all the things that were not going right, I found it easier to apply a quick slap for a minor disciplinary infraction than to do what was loving, gentle and patient. Qualitatively and quantitatively, my girls were never slapped the way I was, but they were slapped, and by my own standard, it was a failure for which I will never forgive myself.

The fact that the Holy Bible seems to condone corporal punishment as both necessary and expected of parents is no comfort for me. As I try to understand why a loving God would prescribe such harsh punishment for children, the dearest and best of humankind, I am forced to remind myself that my unwavering faith in God and his goodness has always existed alongside occasional ambivalence toward the Bible as a wellspring of either infallible wisdom or universal truths. The contradictions seem many and strict fundamentalist interpretations have, arguably, done more harm than good in the world.

As some scholars have pointed out, the book of Proverbs, with its heavy emphasis on corporal punishment, was written by King Solomon. As a child I heard only about the wisdom of this King. As an adult, I have learned that he was not universally revered. For example, Robert Green Ingersoll saw him as "a murderer, an ingrate, an idolater and a polygamist, a man so steeped and sodden in ignorance that he really believed he could be happy with seven hundred wives and three hundred concubines!"[32]

Ultimately, I believe that spanking inflicts unnecessary pain, perpetuates violence, and conveys the impression that it is okay to unleash one's anger and frustration on those who are smaller and weaker. In a world often filled with pain and disillusionment, childhood should be protected and preserved as a consummately bright spot, completely free, innocent and unblemished; it should be a time of incomparable promise and beauty when everything is clothed in wonderment, innocence and delight. Adulthood is time enough for us to discover that life can hurt.

TWENTY-FOUR

On My Own

*I believe that every right implies a responsibility; every opportunity,
an obligation; every possession, a duty.*

—John D. Rockefeller, Jr.

It is countdown to getting her driver's license, as far as Alya
is concerned. At fifteen, she has lived in America for almost
tcn ycars. While there is much of her West Indian heritage that she has
retained, there are many aspects of life in her adopted land that she
takes for granted. The right to get her permit at age fifteen and a half,
in anticipation of a driver's license at age sixteen, is one of them. True
to form, she will not allow my ears to eat grass. I am inundated by her
requests, reminders, questions, plots, plans and schemes to begin the
process the moment she strikes the right age.

I am not so sure.

In Jamaica, would-be drivers cannot acquire a permit until
they turn eighteen—the legal age of adulthood, when an individual
is considered ready to be independent and responsible enough to own
and operate a motor vehicle.

Even so, obtaining a driver's license at eighteen is not a rite
of passage the way getting one at sixteen is here in the United States.
One big deterrent is that in Jamaica, the vast majority of people do not

have the resources to purchase cars for their children at that age, and except for the wealthiest one percent of the population, most young adults do not have access to jobs or capital that would allow them to buy vehicles. For the average person, owning a car is an arduous task, not significantly different from buying a house.

I was in my early twenties before I took driving lessons. My first experience behind the wheel was in a little blue Ford Escort with a big red "L" for "learner" on the back and front bumpers. Mastering the car's ins and outs seemed like one of the hardest things I had ever done. Apart from the fact that it operated manually, it was old and cranky with a mind of its own. Worse, it took me a long time to coordinate my hand and foot movement so that I could put the car into gear, release the clutch, and accelerate before the car shut off completely.

The car shut off countless times on the streets of Kingston. With the big "L" identifying me as not just a learner but a "lunatic" in Jamaican popular culture, learning to drive was not a pleasant experience. It was especially hard at stoplights when I was at the front of a line of vehicles and the car stalled on green.

When it was all over, I was not in a hurry to drive anything, escorted or unescorted. My driver's license became my favorite form of identification and nothing more until I moved to the United States.

It took me seven years here to get a Maryland driver's license. Since I had no car or any aspiration to own one, I learned the metro transit system thoroughly. I loved settling down with my favorite book or newspapers on the subway trains or on the number seventy bus during the long, slow ride from Howard University at the southern end of Georgia Avenue to Silver Spring Station in Maryland. After I moved from my old apartment building—which was within walking distance of the Glenmont Metro at the end of the Red Line in Maryland—I saw the need to buy a car. With two teenagers and a single Ride On bus serving my new neighborhood, getting caught in the rain more than once, and standing in the freezing weather at the bus stop, I felt I had run out of options.

I bought my first car in 2005, a barely two-year-old gold Toyota Camry. Although the Camry is one of the commonest cars on the road,

I believed mine had some special elegance. For anyone driving a late-model black Mercedes, BMW or Saab convertible, this description might seem funny. But for anyone driving an old beat-up car of whatever year, my Camry would have seemed like a dream car. Importantly too, it was one more symbol of my independence and of my capacity to venture into the world and do what I had to regardless of the challenges. Four months later, on January 30, 2005, Alya's fifteenth birthday, I crashed my car less than a block away from my house. She was sitting in the seat next to me. Her scream alerted me that I was heading for the utility pole but it was too late.

Apart from shock, particularly at how easily the car had shredded on impact, I was mostly fine and so was my daughter. My injuries consisted mostly of bruises—contusions, the doctor called them—from my seatbelt cutting into my skin as it kept me from exiting through the windshield. After the accident, I knew more than ever that I was not ready to have my teenager driving anything at fifteen, sixteen, or even seventeen.

I had not been speeding or driving drunk. The road was fine and familiar, and there was no traffic. Experts say most accidents occur under these conditions. A driver, familiar with his or her surroundings can easily become comfortable or distracted—as it was in my case—leading to unfortunate and often fatal accidents.

In addition, most accidents involving teens do not involve drugs or alcohol use. They occur because teenagers lack the experience to judge speed and distance, fail to react appropriately to sudden change, get easily distracted, and lack the experience to drive in the dark and in adverse weather conditions. All of this suggests that teenagers are not psychologically ready or their psychomotor skills developed enough to facilitate the brain-body connection that driving demands.

Most industrialized countries recognize that teenagers are not ready to drive, and that the two years between ages sixteen and eighteen actually make a big difference. In Belgium, China, Denmark, Finland, France, Germany, India, Italy, Japan, Switzerland, The Netherlands, Norway, Portugal, Russia, Spain and Sweden, teenagers are not allowed to drive before age eighteen. In Iceland, Ireland, Poland and the United

Kingdom, the driving age is seventeen. In Australia, with its vast areas of sparsely populated lands, the driving age is staggered between ages sixteen and eighteen depending on population density. The United States and Canada have been the two most liberal countries as far as the legal driving age goes, with teenagers, on average, being able to get licenses at age sixteen.

Here in the United States, there is a clear relationship between the legal driving age and the number of road accidents and fatalities. In fact, road accidents are the leading cause of death for young people between ages sixteen and twenty. Drivers in the seventeen-to-nineteen age group make up nearly sixteen percent of all driver and passenger deaths and eighteen percent of all driver and passenger injuries. The age group with the next highest record of at-fault crashes was the twenty-one to twenty-five year olds. Experts say these data strongly suggests that a new driver takes at least five years to develop the judgment and skills of an experienced driver. Regardless of age, however, the first six months are especially critical for all new drivers.

Maryland has had more than its fair share of teenagers injured or killed on the road. In the four-year period from 1996 to 2000, one out of every ten licensed Maryland teens was involved in a vehicular crash. Further, although teens make up less than six percent of the state's driving population, they comprise almost twelve percent of drivers in fatal crashes, according to Ellen Engleman Conners, who served as Chairman of the National Transportation Safety Board from 2003 to 2005.

Prompted by a rash of tragedies, in 1999 Maryland introduced a graduated driver license system, making it impossible for a teenager to obtain a full license until they are at least seventeen years and nine months. Although they can still get a learner's permit at fifteen years and nine months, the application must be co-signed by a parent or guardian if the teenager is under eighteen, and they must also pass a vision test administered by the state's Motor Vehicle Administration (MVA).[33] Permit holders are allowed to drive only under the supervision of a licensed driver who must be seated up front. Moving violations during this period require the learner to restart the mandatory four-month period. However, successful completion paves the way for a provisional license at the minimum age of sixteen years and one month. To get a provisional license, learners must enroll in a state-approved driver education program consisting of thirty hours in the classroom and six hours behind the wheel. They must also show a MVA skills log signed by a parent, guardian or supervisor attesting that a minimum of a further forty hours of supervised driving practice has been completed. Finally, the new driver must complete a skills test administered by the MVA.

Successful completion of the requirements for the provisional license still comes with a caveat. Learners under age eighteen can drive unsupervised only between 5 a.m. and midnight, except when driving to work, educational activities and official functions. For provisional license holders, a violation requires restarting the eighteen-month minimum period, and driver improvement classes for the first offense. A second offense warrants a thirty-day license suspension and the third, one hundred and eighty days suspension. To obtain a full driver's license, an applicant must have held a provisional license for the preceding eighteen months, and must have no conviction for any moving violations during the provisional license period.

Rite of passage or not, I support Maryland's effort to use its latitude to protect teenagers and I plan to do my part to protect my own: Alya will not drive on her own before age eighteen. I am committed to finding new ways to stall until then.

TWENTY-FIVE

In The Shadow Of Death

Death is not the end
Death can never be the end
Death is the road
Life is the traveler
The Soul is the Guide

—Sri Chinmoy

Oct99ober 2, 2002 was like any other day in my life during the
past ten months. After an uninspiring day at the office,
I rode the Red Line train to Maryland and exited at the Glenmont
station at 6:03 p.m. The last ten to fifteen minutes of my trip would
be on foot regardless of the weather. I exited the Metro Station and
headed toward my apartment on Glenmont Circle, inside the Glenmont
Forest complex.

Effortlessly, my feet took me south on Georgia Avenue, past the
Kentucky Fried Chicken, past the 7-Eleven, across Layhill Road and into
the Glenmont Shopping Center. It was a route so familiar, I could have
walked it with my eyes closed. I had been doing it nearly every day since
the Glenmont Metro Station opened in July 1998.

Normally, my purposeful meandering would be interrupted
by a stop at Magruders, or CVS Pharmacy—just in case we needed

something that I could not think of but would recognize if I saw it on the store shelf.

That evening, I did not stop. I gave the stores a wide berth—walking across the parking lot rather than on the pavements as I would normally. Walking close to the stores was luring me inside. I had decided to avoid that, and the impulse to buy a loaf of bread that we did not need yet.

I had a real job now—I was no longer just a teaching assistant—which meant that I needed to begin to save money. I needed to make plans to get my children out of the apartment and into a house. The complex was changing—more and more itinerant laborers on the steps in the evenings, and more and more trash and empty beer bottles in the mornings.

Five minutes later, 6:08 p.m., I was in front of the new Shoppers Food Warehouse. I cast a baleful glance at the long rectangular building with its new red and yellow logo. Rumor had it that the arrival of this giant retailer meant that Magruders, a smaller, locally operated store, would be checking out. That would not be good as far as I was concerned. I knew everyone in Magruders by face and some of them by name, including several friendly employees from Melwood, an organization serving individuals with disabilities in the Washington D.C. area. I also knew exactly where on the shelves to find everything. I did not want to have to switch to a huge new store with a quarter mile between the produce and the eggs.

Why did Shoppers have to come to Glenmont? Why couldn't the shopping center have turned the big, empty building into a recreation center or a plant nursery?

I looked away from the store toward Randolph Road, and saw yellow police tape, officers in the parking lot and emergency vehicles. A body, wrapped in white and securely fastened with dark colored straps, was on the ground. A small group of curious onlookers watched from outside the tape.

Immediately, I was a reporter again desperately needing to know the story. Police tape meant crime or something untoward, that meant news. It did not matter that I had no editor to report to. I wanted to write a complete story in my head. Plus, this was Glenmont, the little corner of America where I had carved out something of a community for my children and myself. Everything that I needed was in walking distance: the international market where I could find codfish, real yellow yam and plantains from South America and Walkerswood jerk seasoning from Jamaica; Wheaton Regional Library, Wheaton Regional Park and beautiful Brookside Gardens; the train station, the Motor Vehicles Administration; the Immigration and Naturalization Office and even the Internal Revenue Service. I planned to look for a house right there in Glenmont or as close as possible as soon as I had enough money. So, if something was happening right across the street from where I lived now, I wanted to know about it.

A middle-aged African-American woman was pacing the pavement to my left. She was well dressed, sweet faced and distinguished looking with proud traces of gray in thick, mostly black hair.

"What happened?" I asked, walking up to her.

"A man just died in the parking lot—right behind his car. They are saying it was a heart attack," she said her voice sufficiently sad for the victim.

"Oh, how awful!" I said, imagining the pain of a family somewhere who would have to deal with the news that, instead of returning from his shopping trip, their loved one had gone to eternity.

I did not need to know anymore. In the news business, death by natural causes was not much of a news story unless the victim was someone famous or important like the Pope, Mother Teresa or Michael Jackson. I should move on, I thought, to make room for the fallen pilgrim to carry on with dignity on his new journey. Plus, I needed to hurry home to my daughters. I needed to hurry home to hug them long and hard and to tell them that I love them so much—just because I did—and just because simple shopping trips sometimes go frightfully awry.

"I am so sorry," I mumbled to the woman, not knowing what else to say. "I have to go. My children are waiting."

"I want to go too," she said anxiously, "but my car is inside the police tape."

Unwittingly, she was webbed into the process. I was not. I

wished her good luck and continued my pilgrimage across the street, pondering life's fragility and the strange forks in its roads:

Why is there no early warning system to give us a heads up when life is going to end—just so we could tell our families that we love them one last time; just so we could tell them that we would not be home for dinner; just so we could savor a last sundae, or cognac perhaps; just so we could linger for one moment beneath the splendor of a golden moon; just so we could stroll along our favorite stretch of beach to watch the waves crash to the shore; just so we could see the tinges of a sunrise or a sunset on water one last time?

With death or the prospect of it always a constant, how does our mind know to embrace life and not fear its end? How do we know to indulge our laughter and hold our tears at bay? How does one choose to see the silver lining instead of the clouds? Is it not true that as surely as every dark cloud has a silver lining, that there is a big old cloud wherever there is a silver lining?

Just over a year before, on a fall morning drenched in rich, yellow sunshine, I had reason to ponder those same questions.

September 11, 2001, dawned warmer than usual and as splendid as a dream. I took the Red Line train from Glenmont to Union Station and caught the MARC train to Bowie State University where I taught an early morning class as an adjunct professor. The students were not talking much, but they were alert and listening and that, at least, was encouraging. I felt comfortable with the assignment I was outlining to them as the class drew to a close.

Twenty-five minutes after nine. The dean's assistant poked her head around the door. The University's president would be assembling the student body in the auditorium shortly, she said, and I needed to send out my class.

I glanced at my watch. The class was winding down. I would send them out shortly, I responded, not recognizing the urgency in her voice.

"You don't know what is happening, do you?" she asked, suspiciously, her head tilted to one side.

I shrugged. What could possibly be happening? What difference would five minutes make? Students in historically black schools needed every minute of their class time.

"No," I said politely. "What?"

"Our country is under attack," she said. "People are flying planes into buildings...the World Trade Center is down....the Pentagon is on fire...."

Holy Mother of God!

"You are dismissed," I told the class in my most authoritative tone. "Go straight to the auditorium, all of you."

I grabbed my books, chalk and duster and scrambled out behind them toward the tiny office I shared with two other adjunct professors. They were nowhere to be found but one look at CNN confirmed that Mary Lampe had not lost her mind. Plumes of smoke were billowing into the air from what, moments before, had been the World Trade Center. With its signature twin towers, the center consisted of more than thirteen million square feet of office space in the heart of New York City's financial district. Once the tallest building in the world, it had one hundred and ten stories with a lobby six stories high. The towers were the defining feature of the city's skyline.

I watched as CNN replayed the image of two airplanes— suddenly looking like sleek black monsters—slicing through the air and into the sides of the buildings, taking lives and leaving shock and mayhem behind.

America under attack? Why? By whom?

I did not know the answers, but I knew the world was about to change in fundamental ways.

I have to get back to Montgomery County. I have to find my children, came my next desperate thought.

A few hours before, I had sent them off to school but since that time the world had changed in dramatic ways.

Was this Armageddon?

The MARC trains had stopped running by the time I made it to the station across the yard from my office. Frantically, I looked up and down the track, wondering how I was going to make it home, close to thirty miles away. Answers eluded me.

I wandered back to my campus building and got lucky. Two strangers, an African couple, were leaving the building and headed toward their car. I prevailed on them, and they agreed to drop me at the train station in New Carrolton. Metro, surprisingly, was still up and running, and I began a deeply contemplative trip home to Glenmont.

All through the train ride and later the fifteen-minute walk home, I wondered if my children had made it home. I knew that Montgomery County had dismissed school. But unlike many of the kids, they had no one to pick them up and take them home.

They were there, seated on the living room floor watching the tragedy unfold on television, the door tightly locked against the world. I sat beside them, and together, we settled down to sift through the morass of information. For many weeks following, we watched, listened and pondered the nature of life and death, good and evil, war and peace.

—꿈—

A little more than a year later, my casual encounter with death in a supermarket parking lot revived those memories. I did not know then that more mayhem was about to befall our community.

Sometimes death is just what it is—a natural progression of human existence. Sometimes it is a welcome relief from pain and suffering.

Sometimes it is a moment to ponder what lies on the other side: Is it the final parting, or is it merely an exciting new beginning that we do not have the privilege of knowing until we are actually there? Does it open a door to our rewards for how good or bad we were in our lifetime? Is there a heaven—eternal life in paradise—or a hell—eternal damnation—beyond death?

Sometimes death seems too random, too unfair—like when it comes unexpectedly on a glorious fall day, fueled by unfathomable rage at innocent people or at the end of a task as mundane as stocking groceries in the car.

I had no idea who the dead man in the parking lot was and I

would probably never know. Even so, I could not let his life and death go unacknowledged, as if he had not mattered. So I told my children about him briefly, then quickly proceeded to our usual routine: watching *World News Tonight* with Peter Jennings, my favorite news anchor, while I fixed dinner. During dinner, I listened to the girls talk about their day at school and helped them with homework afterward.

By 8:30 that night, they were safely tucked in bed and I began preparing for work the next day. To my dismay, I soon found that every single pair of stockings I owned had runs too big to be concealed by the skirt I planned to wear. I decided on a quick run back to Glenmont Center. For this short errand, the cosmetic section at the reviled Shoppers would have to do since it was closer than the CVS.

The body was still in the parking lot.

I had my first small flutter of unease. The police in America did not work like this. They had working cars and ambulances—lots of them. Plus, the station was right across the street if they needed something more. Why hadn't they removed the body?

Fox Five News at 10 p.m. explained why: The death was a homicide. The lengthy investigation suddenly made sense but I dismissed the incident as an anomaly. Nothing like that had ever happened in the neighborhood before. I could live with one homicide in my neighborhood every five years, I thought.

Noontime, the next day, October 3, I left my office on Georgia Avenue, heading to the main campus at Howard University where I was covering a class. It was in the College of Arts and Sciences—up the infamous Howard Hill—and I had not given myself enough time. I would have to run to make it to Locke Hall before start time at 12:10.

On my way through the lobby of the Howard Center, an item on FOX news at noon caught my attention: Montgomery County schools were under lockdown. Right away I knew that there was a serious security issue but I did not know what, and I could not wait for the recap.

One thing I had learned about Montgomery County, I thought, as I hurried up the hill, was that I could trust the school system. So if my children were locked up in Glenallan Elementary, with the firehouse and police station two blocks away, they were nearly as safe as they could possibly be. I proceeded to teach, confident that my girls were fine even after the ill-advised early dismissal on September 11, 2001.

Near the end of the class, though, I wondered aloud about the newscast.

"Oh, Miss, somebody is driving around shooting people in Montgomery County. They have killed like five people since last night and this morning," one of my students volunteered.

Instantly, my mind went back to the body in the parking lot the night before. My children's school was less than one block east.

I have to get to Montgomery County. I have to get to my children, came the drumbeat in my ears.

"You are dismissed," I said, grabbing my supplies and following the students out of the room.

I did not know then that the night before I had stumbled upon the first victim of a bizarre plot conjured in the twisted minds of a bitter miscreant and a wandering boy. But as more shootings occurred and mayhem descended on our neighborhood, I, along with the rest of the population tried to cheat death at the bus stop, the gas station, on my way to school with the children, or walking back and forth to the store or to Glenmont Metro Station as I had done for years.

For twenty-three days, death was everywhere in our neighborhood, and I was afraid.

I was afraid for myself; I could not die and leave my little girls to face life's vagaries without their mother.

I was afraid for my daughters; they were too young to die. The promises of their beautiful souls had yet to be fulfilled.

By the time the killing spree was over, ten people were dead. The first casualty was James D. Martin, 55—the body I saw in the parking lot. Martin was shot at 6:04 p.m., one minute after I exited the train, four minutes before I arrived on the scene. Five of the victims—James L. Buchanan, 39, of Arlington, Virginia; Prem Kumar Walekar, 54, of Olney, Maryland; Sarah Ramos, 34, of Silver Spring, Maryland: Lori Ann Lewis-Rivera, 25, also of Silver Spring; and Pascal Charlot, 72, of Washington, D.C.—were killed on October 3.

On October 7, panic reached new levels. That day a thirteen-year-old schoolboy was shot and critically injured as he was dropped off at school in Bowie, Maryland. Charles Moose, Montgomery County chief of police, let slip a tear during a news conference on the progress of his investigations, reflecting the collective frustration and fear of more than 800,000 people who call Montgomery County home as well as the hundreds of thousands of others who lived in the Washington, D.C. metropolitan area.

Dean H. Meyers, 53, was killed on October 9 in Manassas, Virginia. Kenneth H. Bridges, 53, was killed on October 11, in Fredericksburg, Virginia. Linda Franklin, 47, was killed in Falls Church, Virginia on October 14. The last victim, 35-year-old Conrad Johnson, a bus driver, was killed on October 22, at 5:56 a.m in Aspen Hill, Maryland, as he stood on the step of his Ride On bus, preparing his paperwork for the day ahead.

Alya, Ilsa and I were frequently in Aspen Hill—home to a Kmart and Home Depot. We sometimes rode the number 26 Ride On there, and to the Seventh Day Adventist Church at Homecrest and Layhill, the bus Johnson was driving that morning. I saw his photo on the news and I knew with certainty that I had seen him before.

Thursday morning, October 24, 2002, the nightmare ended. At 3:19 a.m. John Allen Muhammad, 42, and Lee Boyd Malvo, 17, were arrested as they slept in their car at a rest stop in Frederick County, Maryland. As the story unfolded, the world learned that Muhammad, an ex-military sharpshooter, had been married and divorced three times. Always a little out of control, he became unhinged when he lost custody of his children. Lee Malvo, Muhammad's teenage accomplice, was the son of a Jamaican mother—a single woman whose bid to give him a better life went horribly awry. Moving frequently in search of opportunities, she ultimately took desperate measures to get him to the United States. But more than he wanted the "opportunities" his mother sought to give him, the boy needed a home and a father. Muhammad, meanwhile, needed a pawn. They found each other and thus began the unraveling of two lives.

I felt deep pain for the innocent victims. Too, I felt deep sorrow for the woman who brought Lee Boyd Malvo into the world. Her anguished struggle reminded me of my own, and I empathized with her desires even though I questioned her methods. In many ways, we were on the same journey—struggling to raise our children alone and wanting the best for them. Unfortunately, she lost both her way and the smart, gifted son she loved.

As I contemplated the horror of it all, I deepened my resolve to love my daughters more and better, and moreso never to confuse material gains with security or fulfillment. More than that, I asked God to take my tiny hand in his big ones and never let me lose my way.

TWENTY-SIX

Thy Will Be Done

Death is a commingling of eternity with time.

—Johann Wolfgang Von Goethe

"**M**ommy?"

"Uh?"

"Do you have my power of attorney?"

The question came out of left field, and I marveled at the wonderful insight that I was gaining into the minds of my children. At fourteen, Alya was paying far more attention to me than I was paying to her. More than that, she was applying principles from other people's lives to her own.

My aunt had just died in Brooklyn, New York. She was a stunningly beautiful woman and a central figure in my extended family for as long as I could remember. She lived her eighty plus years with flawless elegance; the rest of us mostly lived in awe of her or accepted that we could never live up to her expectations. We were shocked, therefore, to find after she died, that her affairs were not in order. Her will was fifteen years old, a key beneficiary had predeceased her, she had not named an executor and she made only passing reference to a husband from whom she had been separated for more than thirty years but never divorced. Further, there was no mention of how she wished to dispose of considerable personal effects and, to make matters worse, she had no children—no one figure who would appear to the extended family as the logical choice to take over her affairs. But she had a bunch of warring relatives eager to claim her jewelry, fine crystal and china, beautiful coats, lovely old furniture and quaint *objets d'art.*

Although I was uniquely close to her in some ways, I tried hard to keep out of the confusion and the contention. I saw no dignity in fighting over what I had not worked for and what clearly did not belong to me even with the passing of the rightful owner and the absence of a clear-cut heir. Still, I could not escape it entirely and I was party to several telephone conversations about her estates. The words will, executor and power of attorney came up often.

I had no idea that Alya was paying attention, let alone absorbing the chaotic details of her life. She had never met her great aunt, never spoken to her on the phone or corresponded with her in any way. For all practical purposes, Aunt Aldith and Alya were strangers until the noise of her sudden death entered our house. In the circumstances around my aunt's death though, my daughter saw some uncomfortable parallels to her life.

"Do you have my power of attorney?" she asked, a few days after I came back from the funeral.

"What do you mean?" I asked.

"I mean, if something should happen to me, like I was in the hospital or something, could you sign on my behalf?"

"Yes," I said. "That is automatic because you are a minor."

"Are you sure?" she asked. "What about Daddy?"

"I am not sure," I said quietly, uncomfortably.

Even though the children had lived with me since my relationship with their father ended, I had never gone to court to ask for legal custody and I had never worried about it. Since taking care of the children on a day-to-day basis was entirely my responsibility, I assumed that the right to make key decisions on their behalf was automatic. But as soon as my daughter asked the question, I realized that this was not necessarily so. This was America, not rural Jamaica where decisions are made informally and often more on the basis of custom and tradition than law. Here, the law was written on paper and I had nothing. I had always taken for granted my absolute right to sign on her behalf but maybe I was wrong.

"You better make sure Mommy, because I would hate for something to happen to me and I die because you don't have the right to sign for me."

In the ensuing days and months, the conversation with Alya played over and over in my head, particularly after I did some research and found that she was right. Her father also had parental right, despite my role as sole caregiver. Without the papers, I had no more or less right than he did, unlike my initial assumption. I resolved to get the paper work done but I did so with no great urgency, fearing the entanglement in the court system and the investment of time, money and emotions, all of which were in short supply.

A few months later, Alya revisited the issue from a different angle.

"Do you have a will Mommy?"

"No," I answered shamefacedly.

I had thought about making a will many times before and had even made a half-hearted attempt to record personal information— like social security number, bank accounts, life insurance policies and pension plans—to be given to my sisters…just in case.

I knew that making a will was important especially because I was an ocean away from my parents and most of my siblings. My two sisters in Florida, almost three hours away by air, were my closest relatives in America. Should the worst ever happen, I knew it would be a nightmare for them, should they have to sort through the myriad pieces of paper within which reside the details of my legal life, including house and car papers, retirement benefits and life insurance policies.

Then, there are the intangibles such as where I would want my final resting to be—in Jamaica of course, beside my baby sister Claudia who died *en utero* or beside my grandmother and my uncle Maurice. But, I have never told this to anyone, never said that I wanted to rest in the warm fertile earth, somewhere where my beloved brothers, Richard and Marlon, the two youngest siblings, could plant an evergreen or rosebushes above my head and come to visit me on Christmas mornings as they do Claudia, even though they never knew her. Most importantly, I had not made any binding provisions for what would happen to my children.

Then fourteen and twelve, I did not worry as much as I used to that, if I were gone before they could fully take care of themselves, their lives would be harder than I would ever want it to be. Although they are not yet adults, they are getting closer everyday. Plus, their characters are already formed: they are intelligent and ambitious; they are hard working and tenacious; they are honest and upright; they are not promiscuous and they do not smoke, drink or do drugs and they have a very clear moral framework that allows them to abhor the existence of all three. They know the difference between right and wrong and they have already chosen which side of that great divide they want to be on—the same one I have chosen for them.

Although I have little to leave them financially, I do believe that they would find it within themselves to secure an education and to lead rewarding lives—which is all I want for them. Still, they would be missing a mother—the main buffer between them and the world since the day they were conceived; their staunchest advocate and ally; someone to whom their well-being meant everything; and the person who knows them better than anyone else.

"Shame on you Mommy," Alya said pertly. "You need to make your will."

I looked at her wonderingly. Why was she forcing me to grow up when a part of me was not ready? Why was she trying to make me confront my mortality? How come at her age, she had the courage and common sense that I seemed to lack in middle age?

I knew I needed a will and I had thought about it often enough. It was the mortality thing—the act of giving my final instructions that would make it more real—that was hard. Most of us, me included, avoid confronting our mortality, choosing instead to leave it where it is—at some vague place in the far recesses of our mind. We all know it will surface one day, whether we are ready or not.

Most Americans, I found, die intestate. The two most common reasons for this are people's distaste for confronting the reality of death and the perception that only the wealthy need to make a will.

Actually, making a will is important for everyone over age eighteen for many good reasons. It is the only way to ensure that one's prized possessions go to those one would wish to have them and it is an individual's only chance to appoint an executor to manage his or her estate and ensure that last wishes are carried out. Most importantly, for people with children under age nineteen, making a will allows an individual to choose a guardian for them. Without a chosen guardian, the court will appoint someone who could be the last person a parent would want.

"I would want to go to Auntie Lor," Alya said, bringing my attention back to the moment. "She is more like you than any other person I know. That's why I call her Auntie Mommy."

Auntie Lor, sibling number six, was born Christmas day 1972. I was born on New Year's Day seven years before. This perhaps accounts for the deep metaphysical bond that is beyond that of being sisters. There is something else too. I was a preteen when she was still a toddler. In those years of carrying her on my hips, combing her hair, picking her up and soothing her cuts and bruises, our special bond was formed. Years later, I would see it reflected in my children's relationship with her.

"Auntie Lor would take good care of you," I said quietly.

"I know Mommy. That is why you have to make a will and write it in there. If anything happens to you, I want to go to Auntie Lor."

"I will," I promised. "As soon as I start my vacation, I will tidy up the papers in my drawers, and I will make my will."

"What about you Mommy? If something happened to you, would you want me to resuscitate?"

Lord Jesus.

Like millions of people all over the world, I watched the sad saga of Terri Schiavo. The Florida woman's life became a national drama in 2005 when some legislators sided with her husband to end her fifteen years on life support, while others sided with her parents, who wanted to keep her alive in a "persistent vegetative state."

"It depends." I said. "I don't want them pulling the plug too, too early."

"I would not let them do that," she interrupted quickly.

"But as soon as it becomes clear that I am not coming back, I would want them to. And, I am an organ donor."

"You are?"

"Yes, it's on my driver's license."

"That's cool," she said, and I was happy for that note of admiration—the one that said at least I had done one thing right.

Shortly after that, I took steps to comply with my daughter's request and to do something I should have done a decade and a half before—make a will, appoint an executor and put in writing details of my life that would make the lives of my children, and Auntie Lor, much easier should I fail to live to see one hundred and one.

Women, I found, make up nearly half of people dying intestate. I found out too that estate laws are mostly cast in stone. They are applied strictly and many women's resources sometimes end up just where the deceased did not want them to go—to in-laws they couldn't stand or to an abusive spouse from whom a woman may have been separated but never divorced. In some states in the United States, money earmarked for the deceased's children is controlled by a state-appointed administrator who must be paid a fee until each child turns eighteen. Having a valid will is the only way to prevent all of this.

Making a will is not as hard as it seems. The services of an attorney are not necessarily required, for example. Experts say with a little preparation, most adults can draft a will themselves. Self-help books and software available online, at local bookstores and in most public libraries provide useful guidelines. For a will to be considered binding, however, it must be typewritten or computer generated since not all states honor handwritten wills. Further, the author must state that it is his or her will, must outline decisions about property and the guardianship of minor children if they exist. It must be dated and signed in the presence of two to three witnesses, who must also sign the document.

Finally, a will does not have to be notarized or registered with any government agency to be considered legal. Upon completion, it needs only to be in a safe but obvious place that others (a spouse or children) are aware of. People who find the process too confusing should hire an attorney.

For most of us, the task of making a will will always be difficult because of the sheer psychological weight that it represents. Yet, as distasteful as it may be, it is a gift of thoughtfulness and an act of deep consideration for the loved ones left behind.

For every mother, thy will, like mine, must be done.

TWENTY-SEVEN

These Are My Neighbors

I believe in a different kind of universal
It is a universal rich with particulars
The Deepening of each particular
The coexistence of them all

—Aime Cesaire

"**W**hy do you like Jews so much?"

Sarah, a young Jewish girl from up the street, looked at the fifty cents Alya handed her. Blond and chubby cheeked, she was suddenly flushed with excitement. She still had the books she was trying to sell and she had an extra fifty cents. It was a bonanza for a young colporteur.

Alya did not want the book nor did she want to stop talking on the phone right then. Although she was already a teenager, younger neighborhood children like Sarah sometimes dropped by for a chat or invited her to join in their games. She did sometimes—just to humor them. At other times though, she just wanted to be a thirteen-year-old who did not want to be bothered with nine- and ten-year-olds. This was the case the evening Sarah came trying to sell her books on Judaism while she talked on the phone.

A few days before, we bought lemonade from Mary. She is Jewish too and lives in the house next door to us. Dark-haired, dainty and delightful, she was secretly my favorite of the neighborhood children. Sarah no doubt heard about Mary's success and thought she would try her hand at selling us something too.

Alya, a kindhearted girl who loathes hurting anyone's feelings, ignored the books, dug into her pocket and handed the girl the change, intending to send her on her way with her feelings intact. Sarah, however, wanted to have a conversation.

"Why do you like Jews so much?" she asked, a slightly baffled look on her face.

—⟶⟵—

It was summer 2006. The Middle East was in the throes of a sudden and vicious war between Hezbollah, a radical Lebanese group, and the state of Israel, the spiritual home of Jewish people worldwide, including more than seven million who live there.

I counted myself among the well-thinking people in the world who found this war disappointing not only because of its surface ruthlessness, but because it was happening at all. Hezbollah's kidnapping of two Israeli soldiers ostensibly caused the latest outbreak, but the world knew that it was more a trigger than a cause. The root of the conflict was in centuries-old hostility between some Jews and some Arabs over territorial lands in the Middle East, which both groups claim to be rightfully theirs, and increasingly with differences over religion, culture and ethnicity embedded in the subtext. The cause of the conflict in the last century, however, dates back to political instability at the end of the Ottoman Empire which lasted from 1299 to 1922, and later the 1948 British Mandate, which establishes the modern state of Israel on lands some Arabs believe rightfully belong to them.

The naïve, or the hopelessly idealistic, continues to hope that as time advances, people will come to grips with their common humanity and the desire for wars will ultimately diminish—that the need to affirm the sanctity of *all* life will be stronger than the impulse to maim or murder. As far removed as I was from the Middle East physically, I still felt great sorrow for the innocent lives being lost on both sides of the conflict and for the fact that the search for peace in the region had just been dealt another blow.

When the elephants fight, it is the grass that dies.

The grass in this case often meant lovely young girls like my daughters, or like Mary and Sarah, on either side of the great Jewish-Arab divide.

My neighborhood, Kemp Mill Estates, a subdivision in Silver Spring, Maryland, is predominantly Jewish. That did not matter to me when I decided to purchase my home in the middle of the housing frenzy in 2004.

Every man has an equal right to live and be free
No matter what color or flag, or race, he may be.

I share the philosophy of my countryman, Bob Marley, and I believe in the teachings of Jesus Christ, Gandhi, Marcus Garvey and all those who willingly and readily affirm the value of all life—all those who by precept and example implore us to love our neighbors as ourselves regardless of surface or ideological differences. I am devoted too to that eternal line in the preamble to the United States Constitution:

We hold these truths to be self-evident, that all men are created equal,
that they are endowed by their Creator with certain unalienable Rights, that
among these are Life, Liberty and the pursuit of Happiness.

The only thing that mattered when I contemplated buying the house was that the fixer-upper was just about the only thing I could afford that would allow my children to remain in their old schools, that was close to Wheaton Regional Library, and within walking distance of my beloved Brookside Gardens. Amidst the rough and tumble of my life, I found solace in the darkness of the woods and the abundance of shrubs, flowers, geese, turtles, fish and even the odd snake resident in its fifty acres.

Once I moved to Kemp Mill, I began to understand what life was like living in a community dominated by one ethnic group, and one with significant cultural and religious differences from my own. Suddenly, Yom Kippur, Rosh Hashanah and Hanukkah were no longer obscure holidays on the Montgomery County School calendar; they were being celebrated all around me.

The word kosher became commonplace too. I had to take time out to better understand its meaning because the little children, who routinely darted in my backyard to play on the old swing, stoically refused to eat or drink anything that was not kosher, no matter how much their eyes said they wanted to. I found out that Jewish dietary laws stipulates, among other things, that some animals, including their flesh, organs, eggs and milk, must not be eaten; that animals allowed to be eaten should be killed according to Jewish laws; that all blood must be drained from the meat before being eaten; that fruits and vegetables must first be inspected for bugs; and that meat cannot be eaten with dairy.

Given my new surroundings, I thought it was worth moving beyond a cursory understanding of Jewish culture and belief systems— beyond the fact that this was the ethnic group that Adolf Hitler tried to annihilate. Although he did not succeed, he managed to kill or orchestrate the murder of more than six million people.

As a child, I read *The Diary of Anne Frank* and *The Silver Sword* by Ian Serraillier and I watched the movie *Schindler's List*. Beyond the millions of historic and academic discourse on the subject, these artistic works spoke to the horrible tragedy of the Holocaust and evoked great sadness at the reality of man's inhumanity to man. My move to Kemp Mill Estates revived those memories and transformed the Jews from the "otherworldly" victims of the Holocaust into my neighbors.

—m—

S o, what was it that made Jews, Jews? What is it that made them so reviled by Adolph Hitler and those whom he enlisted to annihilate them? And what was the reason behind the endless hostility between Israel and their Arab neighbors?

Jews are mostly descendants of the Ancient Israelites, but there are some who have converted to this way of life which encompasses culture, religion and ethnicity. Until the late eighteenth century, the term *Jew* was interchangeable with followers of *Judaism*, the religion at the core of what binds the nation together. Haskalah, the Jewish Age of Enlightenment in the late eighteenth century, inspired new thinking; however, it became acceptable for people to consider themselves Jewish without necessarily embracing Judaism. Contemporary usage of the term includes people who practice Judaism and have a Jewish background, people without Jewish parents who have converted to Judaism and people who identify themselves as Jewish by descent but do not practice Judaism.

Judaism began in Ancient Israel between 1213 and 1203 BC. Losing two wars to the Romans forced many Israelites to flee their homeland or risk being sold into slavery. Today, the Jewish population worldwide is approximately fifteen million, the majority of whom live in Israel, the United States, Europe and the greater Middle East. The Jewish community is subdivided into ethnic groups, including Mizrahi, Yemenite, Gruzim, Juhurim, Bene Israel, Bnei Menashe, Cochin and Telugu Jews of India, Romaniotes of Greece, Italkim of Italy, various African Jews, and the Persian Jews of Iran.

—⚏—

I n Kemp Mill, I got used to seeing the men, dressed in black suits and top hats or yarmulke, walking alone or in little groups to and from the synagogues on Friday evenings, on Saturdays, and on special holidays. I got used to seeing the women too, in long dresses, many with strollers or very young children walking to the synagogues. I found it interesting that as in Christianity and Islam, women in conservative

Judaism are subjugated to their menfolk generally, but particularly in the synagogues and in some of the traditions they observe.

Over time I got to know a few of the women.

Mary's mom is a beautiful woman and one of the friendliest people in the neighborhood. She is a teacher and a single mother like me. Apart from Mary, her youngest, she has two boys and, like me, she also struggles to make ends meet. This was a novel thought for me in many ways, a countervailing one already to the stereotypical notion that Jews are universally wealthy.

I made friends with Hannah, a woman in her eighties, or rather, she made friends with me. She stayed inside her house most of the time with her husband of many years, except for those days when she compels herself to stroll ever so slowly down the sidewalks of the neighborhood. She clearly suffered from the loneliness of old age, more so because of her extroverted personality, but her love of life and sense of adventure were still evident in her eyes.

I took Hannah and her husband to lunch one day to make up for the many times I promised her I would stop by and never got a chance to. Over hearty bowls of Irish soup at Wheaton's Royal Mile Pub, I discovered that Joseph, her husband, was not a grouch as I had been told—just a painfully shy old man, happy to live in his wife's shadow.

I confirmed too what I had always suspected about Hannah: She was still a spunky twenty-something at heart trapped in the shriveled, weakened body of an old woman. Unlike most of her neighbors, she did not conform to the traditions of her religion and chose instead to live on the fringes of her culture.

A few doors up the road, Leah lives with her husband and daughter. She was the first one out of her house when I ran my car into a utility pole and sat at the steering wheel slightly dazed—grateful that my daughter and I were safe but stunned by how quickly the car had shredded on impact. Leah was serene, gracious and caring and over time, I talked to her more. I grew to appreciate my Jewish neighbors as just people. I wished that labels played less of a role in how we see each other as citizens of the world—all pilgrims essentially on the same journey.

Perhaps then the war raging in the Middle East would not be at all. Perhaps Israel and Lebanon, two highly religious nations, would be better able to reconcile differences and innocent people on both sides would not so easily become prey to the fanatics from either side. Perhaps the children could go to school in peace, play together, and walk home together. Perhaps mothers would not have to worry about losing their husbands and their sons. Perhaps peace, not war or the constant threat of it, would be the defining ethos in the Middle East.

In the latest salvo, the brutal war of summer 2006, Hezbollah was said to be the provocateur, constantly firing rockets into Israeli territory and threatening the lives of its citizens. But Israel's harsh response unwittingly cast the group as the underdog—David to their Goliath.

Evidently, Sarah, my young neighbor, had absorbed the dynamics and its possible repercussions even in our neighborhood, thousands of miles away, prompting her question to Alya:

"Why do you like Jews so much?"

As strange and unexpected as the question was, Alya had an answer for her—an answer for the ages and one that the warring factions would do well to consider.

"I like *people*, Sarah," she said, "*people*."

TWENTY-EIGHT

Mother, Superior?

An example is often a deceptive mirror, and the order of destiny, so troubling to our thoughts, is not always found written in things past.

—Pierre Corneille

That I am not quite the example I want my daughters to follow came as another belated discovery for me. It is not because I am all that bad but because I want them to be better than I am—to take the best of me and leave the rest behind. Still, my influence as a mother, as it is with mothers generally, is so pervasive I wondered if it would be possible for them to cherry-pick in this way. An incident involving two trash cans one evening allowed me to reflect on this and to understand more deeply the powerful influence that I have on my children, even when my actions are inadvertent.

The trash truck came for the recyclables early that morning. On my way to work, I grabbed the big blue bin and hurried back inside the yard, dropping it over the chain-link fence at the side of the house. In the evening, I would move it to the discreet corner at the back, between the porch and the kitchen, where I normally keep the trash cans, I thought as I headed to my car in the driveway. I came home that evening to find the tall green household bins just over the fence next to the blue one. Ilsa, the first one home, had taken the can from the gate and placed it next to the one I had put over the fence earlier.

"Why did you put it there?" I scolded, thinking she had done a shorthanded job. After all, she knew that was not where the cans belonged. Why hadn't she put all three cans in the corner of the patio, behind the kitchen door?

"Why didn't you put them in the back?" I asked.

"I saw the blue one there, so I put that one next to it," she said.

"I put the blue one there only because I was hurrying this morning," I said. "I wanted to move it from the front, but I did not want to open the gate to go all the way back there."

"Oh," she said with a slightly embarrassed giggle. "I didn't know. I thought that was where you wanted them, so I just put that one there."

"Okay," I said, kicking myself inwardly for my absence of faith in her motives. No one knew better than my children how fastidious I can be. Ilsa was simply doing what came naturally: do things exactly the same way mommy did.

The big picture I saw unnerved me as it did a few years before when Alya, my older daughter, gave me cause to reflect on just how much they were watching, and how closely they were following in my footsteps.

I had done the laundry one day—four loads—running back and forth to the laundry room, three floors down in the basement of our apartment where I lived. Next, I cleaned the apartment with the fury of someone avoiding her thoughts. Then, I left the girls at home and went across the street to get groceries. Since I did not have a car at the time, I walked back home, laden with shopping bags and literally stumbled inside the tiny living room when Alya opened the door.

"Oh, Mommy," Alya said, her voice a mixture of admiration and concern. "You work so hard. When I grow up, I want to be just like you!"

I patted her forehead at a loss for words, while inside my head, I screamed loud enough to wake the dead.

"No my darling, I don't want you to be just like me. That is why I am working so hard. I want you to be better than I am. I want you to have a better life. I don't want backbreaking work to take up so much of your life. I want you to be free to dance, play, live your passions, do the things that will make your soul sing much more than I have done."

—⁓—

When I was young and naïve, I thought following mom's example would be a good thing. Most parents dream that they—rather than peers or media or school or even church—will be the biggest influence on their children.

Generally, we trust our values and we want our children to live them too. We hope we have lived our lives in a way that if they walked in our footsteps, they would be just fine. That is the voice of idealism, which assumes that we were always true to our highest values and that the truth of this is reflected in our life's successes.

Over time and through many challenges, I have outgrown my naïveté. I had no desire to see my daughters repeat many of my life's experiences—not those that I believe would be far less than what I want for them and far less than they deserve. In the process of sharing my life with them, however, I realized that much of what will be passed on will be inadvertent—not intended for them to imitate. It is an experience much like what educators call the hidden curriculum—everything that our children learn from being at school and not just what is taught by a teacher, writing on a chalkboard.

An anecdote I once heard about a mother, her ham and her oven illustrates this principle. The mother would always shave her ham at both ends before putting it in the oven. Her daughter grew up watching her, and as a woman, prepared her ham exactly the same until her daughter, the third generation, asked her why.

"Because that's the way my mother used to do it," the woman said.

"Have you ever asked her why?" the daughter asked.

"No," the woman replied, realizing that she did not have a clue why her mother prepared ham that way.

"Why don't you call her now and ask?"

The woman took the phone and dutifully dialed her mother's number.

"Oh," the old woman replied to her question, "the oven that we had was so small, it just couldn't fit the ham I used to buy, but it could if I shaved it off a little."

"Ma, is that the only reason why you used to shave the ham?" the woman asked, looking at her huge oven.

"Yes, dear. What did you think?"

Sheepishly, the woman hung up the phone and told her daughter what her mother said. After a lifetime almost, she had suddenly realized that what she had learned from her mother about preparing a ham was in no way relevant to her life.

My children have much to learn from me. They can learn that there is dignity in hard work, which is the surest way to get what they want from life absent the lucky few who will win the lottery, inherit a fortune or play professional sports for staggering sums of money. For me, no task is too big, too small or too dirty as long as it means paying my way and relieves me of the burden of accepting a handout. I learned quite early that there is no such thing as a free lunch. Even the most innocuous gift often comes with a price. Expectations and conditions, spoken or unspoken, can far outweigh the value of the handout itself.

My children can learn from me how to follow their dreams. My determination has taken me out of abject poverty to a career in journalism in Jamaica, given me the ability to pay my way and the unquantifiable, unimaginable, immeasurable opportunity to be in the same room with Nelson Mandela, the great anti-apartheid leader and one of the most magnificent figures of our time.

My children can learn from me never to be uncertain of their place in the world, never to allow themselves to be defined by others— especially on the basis of race, gender, ethnicity or circumstances they cannot control.

My life has taught me that being oneself can be a struggle. Nonetheless, my faith in myself has always been absolute. I have tried to pass that on to my daughters, and I see it in the calm, all-embracing way in which they relate to the world. More than anything, this acceptance of themselves as children of the universe will determine the extent of their successes in life.

But there are other aspects of my life that I would not want to see repeat in theirs. I pray, for example, that even as they aspire to be their best, they will take life less seriously; that they will do what they must but with a sense of humor and a little less concern for the future because life will be what it will be. I pray that their strength of spirit will enable them to laugh in the face of adversity, because truly what does not take their lives will only make them stronger.

I pray that they will take better care of their bodies and accept, even grudgingly, that in our society physical appearance matters. Although good health should be the primary motive to eat right and exercise, for example, I have come to appreciate that there is no harm in looking good for its own sake. By this I mean clean bodies including teeth, nails and hair; healthy and well-cared-for skin, clean shoes and attractive well-cared-for clothes. To the extent that that conformity is harmless and may help them to accomplish some desired goal, I would urge them to conform. In everything else, I hope that they will have the courage to be themselves.

I pray too that they will be more careful in their relationships, especially with the opposite sex—that they will be more discriminating, stay true to their values and never confuse superficiality with significance. For example, I trust that they will not be afraid to pick the short guy or the one who may not fit the norm, but is a decent human being. For when it comes to men and relationships, what matters is not his education, the size of his bank account—the size of anything else he may have—or what he looks like. What matters is his character— that he is decent, honest, has integrity, respects himself and others and respects values like loyalty, punctuality and hard work. If he has character, he can be trusted to do what matters, including being a good partner and taking care of his family and other responsibilities. Without these things, no matter what else he has, life with him will be hell. More than anything else, I would not like to see my daughters raising their children as single mothers. I would love to see each one in a stable heterosexual union, raising their children with a mature, caring and committed companion.

I pray that they will be systematic and careful about their career choices, especially if they intend to be wives and mothers. In my heart, I would like to say follow your passion, but sometimes what matters most is what is practical—whatever will allow them the flexibility to take care of family in the best possible way.

But is it possible for our children to take some things from our lives as mothers and not others? Some experts say children are influenced mostly from learned experiences but that behavior is generally modifiable. Some even argue that parental influence is actually quite limited, compared to other factors from the larger societal culture, passed on through peers, media, school and other social organizations. Additionally, parents do not control their children's innate characteristics, the choices they make as they grow older or the chance events they will encounter. Other experts believe that most behaviors are innate and therefore fixed and unchangeable. Although our examples as parents may be just one of many influences on children's development, in my opinion, it is one of the most important.

It is uncanny how much of myself I see in my children—the good parts mostly—thank God. At every opportunity, I urge them to emulate the best of me. The ugly parts, they can skip. Like the trash cans at the side of the house, those were inadvertent and never meant to be seen at all.

TWENTY-NINE

Am I My Sister's Keeper?

I don't believe the accident of birth makes people sisters or brothers.
It makes them siblings. Gives them mutuality of parentage.
Sisterhood and brotherhood is a condition people have to work at.

—Maya Angelou

"Where is Abel thy brother?" the Lord asked Cain, firstborn son of Adam and Eve.

"Am I my brother's keeper?" Cain responded flippantly.

"The voice of thy brother's blood crieth unto me from the ground," the Lord said, knowing already that Cain had murdered his sibling.[34]

The story, recorded in the Book of Genesis, is mankind's first murder and it is that of one sibling by another. This watershed moment in man's tenure on earth is a reminder of how difficult the relationships between siblings can be. Our sisters and brothers can be our most loyal friends and companions, but this is not always the case. Jealousy between sisters can arise over anything from a coveted vase to a boyfriend. Brothers too can be fiercely competitive, sometimes destructively so, over career accomplishment or whatever they value as symbols of success. Competition for the favors of relatives, usually parents, can also make the relationship between siblings difficult to navigate.

There are different interpretations of why Cain killed Abel. The most common is that he was jealous because he thought God favored Abel. Both brothers had presented sacrifices to God. Abel, a shepherd, gave to God the firstborn of his flock as well as milk. Cain gave fruits and grain. While God was pleased with Abel's offerings, he rebuked Cain, prompting his rage at his brother. Some theologians suggest that Cain had another motive for killing Abel. Both had twin sisters, whom they were to marry, but Abel's betrothed was the more beautiful. Others suggest that Cain harbored a deep envy of Abel's livestock, and some think Cain was inherently evil.

There are other Biblical stories of sibling rivalry: In Genesis, Jacob, the son of Isaac and Rebekah, tricked his twin brother Esau out of his inheritance and sought refuge away from home under the threat of death. This resulted in many years of enmity. Sisters Rachel and Leah led complicated lives as the wives of Jacob. The discomfiture is hard to imagine as Jacob was tricked into marrying Leah instead of Rachel, whom he loved.

Later in Genesis, Joseph, Jacob's son, became a victim of sibling rivalry. According to the story, Jacob loved Joseph more than all of his children "because he was the son of his old age."

He made him a coat of many colors. And when his brethren saw that their father loved him more than all his brethren, they hated him, and could not speak peaceably unto him.[35]

As the third of eleven children and mother of two, I know how challenging and how rewarding these relationships can be. Oddly enough, it was often easier for me being one of eleven children than it has been being mother of two.

Alya and Ilsa, only twenty-two months apart, are better children than I hoped for. They are smart young women who, since kindergarten, have placed school, service and learning at the center of their lives. They are kind and compassionate, honest, curious about and respectful of all their worlds—physical, social and spiritual. Beyond their normal struggles—they think cleaning their rooms is the same thing as torture and cleaning the kitchen, a crime punishable with eternal damnation—my biggest problem raising them has centered around their intense rivalry at times.

Psychologists say the nature of family life overall, and the relationship between siblings in particular, makes it almost impossible to avoid rivalry. Scientist and educator William Antonio Boyle argues that sibling rivalry is everywhere in nature: the biggest baby shark eats its siblings in its mother's womb in order to secure all available nourishment for itself; baby eagles destroy their siblings for the same reason. Among human beings, children compete for their parents' time, attention, love and approval. The more children there are, the more intense the competition is likely to be.[36]

Jeffrey Kluger, in the *Time* Magazine article, "The Science of Siblings,"[37] argues that the interaction among siblings, outside of birth order, has much to do with the individual's personality. He quotes psychologist Daniel Shaw of the University of Pittsburgh who says that parents serve the same big-picture role as hospital doctors on grand rounds, while siblings are like the nurses on the ward—there every day and therefore the biggest influence on behavior outcome. Shaw concludes that "all that proximity breeds an awful lot of intimacy—and an awful lot of friction."

In the same article, Laura Kramer, professor of family studies at the University of Illinois at Urbana-Champaign, says, on average, siblings in the three-to-seven age group will clash three and a half times in an hour, while those in the two-to-four age group clash more than one time in every ten minutes. Overall, Kramer concluded, getting along with a sibling can be a frustrating experience.

The rivalry between Alya and Ilsa has been exacerbated by the fact that their personalities are so different. Alya is outgoing and fun-loving; Ilsa is serious, studious and somewhat pensive. Alya is carefree and somewhat haphazard; Ilsa is methodical and meticulous. Alya is unapologetically messy; Ilsa is neat and tidy. Alya loves the spotlight, Ilsa is sedate and self-contained. Ilsa likes stability, predictability and order; Alya is happy in the midst of chaos and adept at adapting to her surroundings. Alya is air; Ilsa, earth. Alya is fire; Ilsa, water.

The differences were always there and as they grew into their pre-teen years, they became more pronounced especially as both are natural leaders and tough and unrelenting in different ways. Amidst their frequent clashes, I searched psychology, like birth order theory, for an explanation. I drew a blank. Alya is not interested in excessive order as firstborns are supposed to be. Ilsa, the younger, more closely resembles the profile of the firstborn, according to the theory.

I often felt caught between them in their epic struggles. Each will argue vociferously and convincingly. I felt both helpless and hapless in the face of their demands that I do something about the other. Not knowing what to do much of the time, I often contemplated just retreating to my room and let them work out their differences—so long as there was no hitting—*ever.*

I was never able to take one child's word over the other, never able to discern which one was not quite telling the truth. Only as they grew into their teen years, did I begin to appreciate that although they both had a deep moral core, one was a little more manipulative than the other. For that one, the temptation to tell a white lie to get her way was harder to resist.

The room that they shared in the apartment where we lived until they were eleven and thirteen was a study in contrasts: Ilsa's side was always carefully made up while Alya's looked like a mini cyclone had passed through. That and the fact that they had to share one closet was the source of many conflicts and a constant headache for me.

"I want my own room!" Ilsa declared for a gazillionth time.

I sat her down and told her a story.

—〰—

My parents had eleven children—six boys and five girls. I am number three, with an older sister and an older brother. The three of us began our lives in a tiny, one-room house without closets or indoor plumbing. Our few "good" clothes were hung in a corner of the room in a makeshift closet and our underclothes kept in a trunk, slightly bigger than the footlockers that freshmen pack to take to college. Later, my father built us a three-bedroom house, and later he added a fourth but the babies kept coming too. There was never enough space for anybody to have their own room. Until I was eighteen and went off to college, I shared a room with one or more of my siblings. In fact, I never had my own room until after I graduated college and got my first job. But I have no recollection of fighting with my siblings over space, and not once did I fight with my roommate at college.

Perhaps the reason we never fought was because there was nothing to fight over. Essentially, we needed space on the bed to sleep at nights and that was it. We mostly lived outside and came inside only to be out of the rain or darkness. My daughters, by contrast, had too much. We made too many trips to Kmart, Walmart, Target and Toys R' Us, and they got too much stuff they did not need as birthday or Christmas presents or other occasions. There was just too much stuff crammed into their bedroom.

Yet, by American standards I was poor and my children were growing up in poverty. Compared to most of their friends from Middlebridge, Tivoli and Layhill, who had their own rooms in four- or five-bedroom houses—and whose parents worked for the federal government, were scientists at the National Institutes of Health or attorneys at big D.C. law firms—my girls had very little. Still, they had vastly more than my siblings and I, combined, had as children. Perhaps the problem was not that the room was too small; it was that they had too much stuff.

"But I hate her!" Ilsa routinely declared.

I told her another story.

—⚹—

As a young girl, I helped out with my younger siblings as best as I could. I carried them on my neck or on my back when their little feet were too tired on their way to school or wherever they were going. I washed and soothed their bruises. I bathed them, combed their hair and brushed their teeth. I took them to the free clinics if they needed to go. I went with them on the first day of school and I scrutinized their report cards to make sure they were doing well.

I helped out because I loved their sweetness and innocence; because I understood that we were joined by an irrevocable bond of blood and parentage. And, I helped out because I was sorry for the circumstances in which they were born through no fault of their own— abject poverty with too little to go around to ensure that they would never endure hunger; that they would always go to school and that their potentials as human beings would be fully realized.

Miraculously, they have all done well. They are productive members of society and they have never forgotten how, within the limits of my situation, I tried to be a good sister and took care of them. Now, they are my best friends and they are great aunts and uncles to my daughters—the warring siblings.

"I was never mean to them," I told Ilsa. "There was never any bad feeling between my siblings and me for the most part. Now, you get that back in the quality of loving and caring that they give to you as uncles and aunties."

"But your sisters and brothers are good people."

"So is your sister. She is kind and loving and she does look out for you," I said. "Just think about it. Apart from your parents, she is the closest person you have on earth. She should be your best friend. Both of you came from the same place—from inside your mother's stomach. Doesn't that count for something?"

"I suppose."

"Yes, it does. It's called blood family, and no matter how many friends you have, blood ties supercede that. Don't ever forget: blood is thicker than water."

THIRTY

The Music Of Life

Optimists enrich the present, enhance the future, challenge the improbable and attain the impossible.

—William Arthur Ward

The older I get, the more I realize that life is a lot like driving: before one can safely move forward, one has to check the rearview mirror. December 31st, 1999 was like that for me. It was a critical juncture in time. Humankind was not just beginning a new year but a new millennium. Given the advances in technology, communication technology in particular, I imagined that the new millennium would coincide with many exciting changes in the world.

New Year's Eve found me on a Florida highway in the mother of all traffic jams, along with my sister, the children and my cousin who was driving us to the train station. Everything in the world with four wheels seemed to be sitting on the highway from Orlando heading south. Nothing moved, or showed any sign of moving. Instead, folks were getting out of their cars to stretch their legs or to videotape the ocean of vehicles stretched as far as the eyes could see. Others strolled around. They knew they were not going anywhere anytime soon, their attitude seemed to say, so may as well enjoy the scenery.

I was becoming increasingly edgy. I had a train to catch back to

South Florida and I did not want to miss it.

Helplessly, I sat back and reflected on where I was and where I wanted to be in the year ahead. Doing some mental housecleaning and envisioning for myself was a good way to pass the time. Uppermost in my mind was my status as a single mother, why my relationship with my children's father had ended and how I was going to raise my children alone.

It took me years to summon enough courage to move forward alone. When the end came, I breathed a sigh of relief. But it was relief coupled with deep pain, more so for my children than for myself. I learned then that the death of a dream—that of a happy life with my children and their father—could be one of life's most painful experiences.

As most women in my situation would have done, I found myself deeply engaged in the post mortem—trying to assess how and why everything went so wrong; why my life, manifested in this relationship, had taken such an unseemly turn.

The answer was simple. The seeds of its downfall were always there—sowed from the very beginning. The time spent together was opportunities for those seeds to germinate into anger, disillusionment and betrayal—the death knell for a union that truly was never meant to be.

Still, I had worked hard to save it. In some twisted ways, staying was easier than the alternative, even though I was rarely happy or content with the way things were.

Staying was easier than feeling like a failure at the one thing I wanted to succeed at most. It was easier than explaining to everyone who mattered that I was about to make a decision with long-lasting and profound implications for my life.

It was easier than having to confront the fear of being alone.

It was easier than having to confront the financial challenge posed by my one small income instead of two.

It was easier because I would not have to break my children's hearts.

Yet, in each of our lives, there comes a time when we have to take the alligator by the snout. I began to realize that leaving is the right thing when, rather than being a refuge for family, home is a place filled with toxic fumes.

It is the right thing when we recognize that regardless of wars and rumors of them, of famines, floods and rumors of them, of the struggles and indignities that make our situations challenging at times, life was meant to be beautiful—filled with love and laughter and joy and peace.

Most importantly, leaving was the right thing for my children, who would be most profoundly impacted by the emotional temperature in the home—their first and last line of defense against the world.

I wanted my girls' home to be the place where they learn the beauty of life as well as the skills to help them climb life's mountains. I wanted their home to be their shelter from the storms of life—the place where they could use their training wheels for as long as it took them to find their balance and take off on their own. Indeed, as a teacher and a mother, I fully agree with the adage that children live what they learn:

> *If they live with hostility, they will learn to fight.*
> *If they live with honesty, they will learn truthfulness.*
> *If they live with fairness, they will learn justice.*
> *If they live with kindness and consideration, they will learn respect.*
> *If they live with security, they will learn to have a place in the world.*
> *If they live with acceptance and friendship; they learn to find love in the world.*[38]

As their mother, I was responsible for giving them a home. Further, it was up to me, as much as possible, to shield them from harmful and negative situations and to create for them an uplifting and inspiring environment.

My mind raced with the intensity of my life's issues. The day spent at Disney's Magic Kingdom was over. We had skipped the nighttime celebrations and were trying instead to get back to my sister's home in Fort Lauderdale. The next day, my birthday, would be the start of a new millennium. I wanted to be with my sister and my children, not the hordes of strangers in the theme park. But it looked as if we were going to miss the last train out.

Alternately, I lost myself in thoughts and groaned my frustration at everyone who thought that it was their sacred duty to be on the road on New Year's Eve.

Suddenly, from a car stereo and above the monotonous hum of white noise came pure sweet reggae music. It reverberated through the air, loud enough for everyone to hear many, many car lengths away:

> *Don't worry about a thing,*
> *cause every little thing gonna be all right.*
> *Singin: don't worry about a thing,*
> *cause every little thing gonna be all right!*
>
> *Rise up this mornin,*
> *Smiled with the risin sun,*
> *Three little birds*
> *Pitch by my doorstep*
> *Singin sweet songs*
> *Of melodies pure and true,*
> *Sayin, (this is my message to you-ou-ou:)*

Timelessly reassuring, Bob Marley's words pierced the intensity of my thoughts. It seemed as if my mystic compatriot was reaching out to only me. I wanted to hop out of the car and dance; to float on the lyrics to the world beyond, to reach across time and the universe and hug him to me. I settled for just getting on bad inside the car—to the consternation of my children. I clapped my hands and laughed out loud. I sang alongside Bob's honeyed tones, reveling in music's purest sound; in the wonderful, joyous heritage from whence I came; in the indomitable spirit of my people; in their infamous audacity—for surely, it had to be a Jamaican who was playing that music so damned loud on a U.S. highway, thousands of miles from home.

The music reminded me of the strength of my spirit—the determination to look the biggest challenge in the face without shrinking; the determination that obstacles will not be my excuse, because if I cannot get through it, then I must get over it, under it, or around it, and if all else fails I can use a sledgehammer, blast it to smithereens and keep on going.

This is the spirit of my mother, a peasant woman who used the depth and breadth of her spirit to shield her eleven children from poverty and other forces of darkness prevalent in a poor, rural, post-colonial society; it was the spirit of Queen Nanny, the runaway slave whom Jamaican folklore said was so fierce, so determined, so skilled, that she caught the bullets from the Englishmen's guns, tossed the bullets back at them and slew them. It was the spirit of Harriet Tubman, the great American conductor on the Underground Railroad, who admonished the slaves she was smuggling to freedom:

> *If you hear the dogs, keep going.*
> *If you see the torches in the woods, keep going.*
> *If they're shouting after you, keep going.*
> *Don't ever stop. Keep going.*
> *If you want a taste of freedom, keep going.*

—〰—

The train was late by more than an hour and still, we just barely made it. We scrambled aboard, minutes before it snaked its way out of the station toward South Florida.

And so it was that, as the curtain slipped down on the last day of 1999, I found myself on a journey, literally and symbolically, with my three dearest—Alya, Ilsa and my sister whom they call "Auntie Mommy."

I looked at them with quiet gratitude, and then out the window as the train rumbled on through Florida's Orange County...rumbled into tomorrow.

It was infinitely fitting that the four of us were on that journey together. There was no rancor, no bitterness, no anger, only this quiet reassurance that we would always be there for each other no matter what.

Beneath clouds tinged a mysterious deep violet and alongside trees tinted burnt gold in the rays of a dying sun, the train rumbled on. Through the window, Orange County's numerous lakes stared back at me, meeting my questioning gaze with calm reassuring ones of their own. Inside my head, the music of life played on.

Every little thing gonna be all right.

I wrapped myself in the comfort of yet another lesson learned: life will always have traffic jams. There will be times when we feel like we are stuck in neutral, unable to move in any direction. It doesn't matter how impossible things may seem—how clogged our lives may be with challenges—bills to pay, an unexpected event that disrupts our lives, a divorce or separation and hearts broken into millions of little pieces.

Ultimately, the bottlenecks will clear and if they do not, we will simply follow the detour sign and take another route to where we most want to be. There will be different sceneries, different experiences no doubt, but it will be the same earth runnings.

So, in the midst of life's inevitable traffic jams, take a deep breath. Take a walk. Chill. Listen to the music inside your soul:

Every little thing gonna be all right...

GRACE NOTES

All parents damage their children. It cannot be helped. Youth like pristine glass absorbs the prints of its handlers. Some parents smudge, others crack, a few shatter childhoods completely into jagged little pieces, beyond repair.

—Mitch Albom

Thus asserts best-selling author, Mitch Albom. I concur. I did not give my daughters the "perfect" life I had imagined. Ultimately though, I hope that I have loved them more than I have hurt them; that I have soothed more than I have scolded; that I have expressed my pride and joys more than I have my disappointments; that I have taught them more about courage than about fear and more about laughter than tears. And, I hope that even the moments of imperfections have been lessons learned—lessons upon which to build better experiences for themselves.

Already, I have seen their unfolding in multiple ways.

In 2006, in the semi darkness of the American Film Institute (AFI) Theater in Silver Spring, I cried tears of joy as I watched a poised and confident Ilsa co-moderate Final Conference 2006, a wonderful production of the Montgomery County Arts and Humanities Magnet Program at Eastern Middle School in Silver Spring, Maryland.

I cried for the display of innocence and wholesomeness among my daughter and her classmates—qualities I sometime fear no longer exist in the face of the modern-day sophistry and cynicism of many teenagers.

I cried for the idealism and promise of youth, and for the hopeful new world implicit in the dreams and foresight of my daughter's generation.

I cried because Ilsa earned her way into, and through, the program; because the teachers at Eastern held her to a high standard, demanding always that her performance be in tandem with her capabilities.

I cried because she stood there in defiance of the stereotype of what she is supposed to be as the child of a mother who is poor, single, immigrant and black—all the variables that are supposed to produce at-risk, failing and under-achieving children.

I cried at the culmination of three years of dogged determination and hardwork that was unfolding so magnificently before my eyes. The sacrifice was entirely worth it, I realized.

After testing as gifted and talented in the second grade, Ilsa went on to test into the middle school magnet program where she enjoyed three great years before moving on to the International Baccalaureate (IB) program at Richard Montgomery High School in Maryland. In 2006, she received a scholarship from the Oxbridge Foundation and spent a month at Oxford University. The following year, on a part-scholarship from Tufts University, she spent a month in France in pursuit of her interest in French and international relations. She loved Oxford, and yearns to go back one day. By God's grace... she will.

Alya is now 18 and has just completed her first children's book— *Beatrice, The Ladybug.* She successfully completed her IB program at Our Lady of Good Counsel High School. Despite her struggles, it was mostly a good experience for her—one that I would not hesitate to have her repeat. In the spring of 2008, she had the opportunity to spread her wings when she traveled with her school to Dublin, Ireland. She has just completed her freshman year at the University of Maryland at College Park, where she made the dean's list. She plans to do a semester abroad in Argentina in her sophomore year to further her mastery of the Spanish language and her interest in the history and development of Latin America and the Caribbean. She plans to get her driver's license this summer with my full support. Overall, both girls are fully integrated members of the Montgomery County Community and are active in volunteer work.

Of course, one of our crowning experiences in the United States as a family was witnessing the election of Senator Barack Obama as president of the United States. I watched with keen attention and the deepest sense of satisfaction as the Obama family began the journey to the presidency. I especially identified with Michelle Obama, and I am proud to hold her up to my daughters as another example of the strength and tenderness of authentic womanhood.

On January 20th, 2009, I waved on Ilsa on her pre-dawn jaunt to the National Mall to watch the inauguration of President Obama. I followed hours later to find that the Mall was at capacity and therefore closed to the public. I wound up watching from the warmth, comfort and elegance of the Cannon House Office Building, the oldest congressional office. Like my visits to the White House, it was another experience that made me feel as American as apple pie. Alya chose to stay snug under her blanket and joined her friends at noon to watch it on a big-screen TV.

The girls are now on the verge of being fully independent. Nowadays, we diverge but often converge again to celebrate and explicate.

The journey continues thankfully, still with more good days than bad, but even the bad ones, we have learned to take in stride. We must. It is a part of the tapestry of our lives as mothers, families and human beings.

Notes

Notes

Notes

End Notes

[1]   See St. Luke 15:4 of the King James Version of the Holy Bible.

[2]   Chief Seattle, who lived from 1786 to 1866, was a leader of the Suquamish and Duwamish Native
      American tribes in what is now the U.S. state of Washington. His speech was said to have been
      made in 1854 in reply to a government offer to purchase tribal lands. It is considered as the
      greatest statement on the environment ever written and was introduced to me in that context.

[3]   More information on missing and exploited kids is available at the National Center of Missing
      and Exploited Children at www.missingkids.com; the National Incidence Studies for Missing,
      Abducted, Runaway and Thrownaway Children (NISMART) at www.ncjrs.gov; and from
      Operation Look Out at www.operationlookout.org.

[4]   The American Academy of Pediatrics provides comprehensive information on breastfeeding on
      their website: http://www.aap.org/healthtopics/breastfeeding.cfm

[5]   See Reminiscences by Julia Ward Howe, 1899, p.328

[6]   The statement is attributed both to Ann Marie Reeves Jarvis and to her daughter Anna Jarvis.
      See the Legacy Project at www.legacyproject.org and the West Virginia Genealogy Project at
      http://www.wvgenweb.org/taylor/mothersday/founder.htm

[7]   The International Vegetarian Union provides a list of famous vegetarians on its website—
      www.ivu.org/people. See also the website of the American Dietetic Association at
      www.eatright.org for information on the benefits of a vegetarian diet and the Natural Healing
      Center at www.naturalhealingcenter.com.

[8]   The term has its genesis in Traditional Marxist thought. According to this ideology, religion
      serves the interest of the society's ruling class since it serves to numb the pain of the poor and
      oppressed with the promise of a better life after death.

[9]   See Rev. 21:1-4 in the King James Version of the Holy Bible.

[10] See 1 Cor. 15: 51-54 in the King James Version of the Holy Bible.

[11] Frantz Fanon was a psychiatrist and activist from the French Caribbean Island of Martinique.
      See his 1967 work, Black Skin, White Masks, p. 143

[12] The style originated during the reign of Napoleon I in France and was intended to idealize his
      leadership and the French state. It follows the Louis XVI period in France and corresponds with
      the Federal style in the United States. Among other features, French Empire Style furnishing is
      characterized by: a heavy masculine look; highly polished wood veneers; wood back chairs with
      upholstered seats; the use of designs inspired by classical Greece; and the use of motifs inspired
      by Ancient Egypt, Rome and Greece.

[13] This style of architecture and furnishing occurred in the United States between 1780 and 1830.
      It was associated with the early Republic and the establishment of national institutions of the
      United States and reflected the nation's interest in the ancient democracies of Greece combined
      with the values of Ancient Rome. The Federal style favors symmetry and balance in designs;
      pastel colors in shades of greens, yellows and blues or deep red and sapphire; and upholstery in
      silk with damask pattern. Oval or circular-shaped rooms were a common feature as well.

[14] From www.Economist.com. May 17, 2006.

[15] For current statistics on violence against women visit the World Health Organization at
      http://www.who.int/features/factfiles/women/en/index.html

[16] Planned Parenthood gives nine reasons why abortion should be legal. The citation, in part,
      constitutes choice number nine, which deals with women's right to choose how they live. Their
      web site, www.plannedparenthood.org, provides information on abortion rights and other issues
      relating to women's reproductive health.

[17] See. Exodus 20: 3-17 in the King James Version of the Holy Bible.

[18] See St. Matthew 5: 3-9 in the King James Version of the Holy Bible.

[19] See Matthew 7: 12 in the King James Version of the Holy Bible.

[20] Simon LeVay is an American neuroscientist. He has studied and written extensively on the structure of the brain and human sexuality. His writings can be found on his website: www.simonlevay.com

[21] For example, Romans 1:26-27 states: "For this cause God gave them up unto vile affections: for even their women did change the natural use into that which is against nature: And likewise also the men, leaving the natural use of the woman, burned in their lust one toward another; men with men working that which is unseemly, and receiving in themselves that recompense of their error which was meet." And, in 1 Corinthians 6:9, The Apostle Paul wrote: "Know ye not that the unrighteous shall not inherit the kingdom of God? Be not deceived: neither fornicators, nor idolaters, nor adulterers, nor effeminate, nor abusers of themselves with mankind."

[22] See "Closing the Gap" by Sonja Steptoe in *Time* magazine, November 22, 2004

[23] The College Board is a not-for-profit membership association founded in 1900. The organization administers programs such as the SAT, the PSAT/NMSQT, and the Advanced Placement Program.

[24] For comprehensive data on sexually transmitted diseases in the United States visit the Center for Disease Control at http://www.cdc.gov/std/default.htm

[25] See "Correlates of College Students Binge Drinking by H. Wechsler, G. W. Dowdall, A. Davenport and S. Castillo in the American Journal of Public Health, Vol. 85, Issue 7, 921-926,1995

[26] The statement references the agenda-setting theory of media effects, specifically the 1983 work, *The Press and Foreign Policy*, by Bernard Cohen. Cohen and scholars of similar views believe that by focusing on certain issues above others, the media guide our attention to those issues.

[27] See the 1999 Human Development Report, p.29.

[28] See "Keeping Internet Predators at Bay" at www.usatoday.com/tech/columnist/ edwardbaig/2003-01-29-baig-safety_x.htm.

[29] See Internet Child Sexual Predators at www.crisisconnectioninc.org/sexualassault/Internet_ child_sexual_predators.htm.

[30] The custom of erecting a Christmas tree, usually an evergreen species decorated with lights, is a pagan tradition dating back to 16th century Germany. The tree has no connection to the birth of Christ and no significance in Christianity. It was intended to symbolize the continuation of life throughout the bleakness of winter.

[31] See the 2003 work, *Black and Not Baptist: Nonbelief and Freethought in the Black Community*, by Donald R. Barbera, p. 80.

[32] Robert Green Ingersoll, a veteran of the American Civil War and prominent public leader, was also a well-known agnostic of his time. He advocated free thinking and humanism and often made fun of religion.

[33] For information on requirements for a Maryland Driver's license, visit the state's Motor Vehicle Administration website at http://www.marylandmva.com/DriverServ/APPLY/default.htm.

[34] See Genesis 4:1-16 in the King James Version of the Holy Bible.

[35] See Genesis 37: 3-4 in the King James Version of the Holy Bible.

[36] W.A. Boyle's essay, "Sibling Rivalry," was published on the web in 1999. See full text at http://www.angelfire.com/md/imsystem/.

[37] See "The New Science of Siblings," *Time* magazine, July 2, 2006

[38] The lines come from the poem "Children Learn What They Live," written by Dorothy Law Nolte, a family life educator, in 1954 for the now defunct *Torrance Herald*, a Los Angeles County newspaper. Originally written to fill Mrs. Nolte's weekly family advice column, the poem is revered around the world and has been reprinted in more than 30 languages